THE THEORY OF CONTESTABLE MARKETS

Recent Titles in
Contributions in Economics and Economic History

War in the World-System
Robert K. Schaeffer, editor

Fundamentals of the Economic Role of Government
Warren J. Samuels, editor

Economic Models and Methodology
Randall G. Holcombe

Information Technology and Global Interdependence
Meheroo Jussawalla, Tadayuki Okuma, and Toshihiro Araki, editors

Corporate Hegemony
William M. Dugger

Taiwan's Development: Implications for Contending Political Economy Paradigms
Cal Clark

Income Inequality in the United States, 1947–1985
Nan L. Maxwell

Evolution of United States Budgeting: Changing Fiscal and Financial Concepts
Annette E. Meyer

Charitable Giving and Government Policy: An Economic Analysis
Jerald Schiff

Economic Law and Economic Growth: Antitrust, Regulation, and the American Growth System
George E. Garvey and Gerald J. Garvey

The Politics of Industrial Recruitment: Japanese Automobile Investment and Economic Development in the American States
Ernest J. Yanarella and William C. Green, editors

The Theory of Contestable Markets

APPLICATIONS TO REGULATORY AND ANTITRUST PROBLEMS IN THE RAIL INDUSTRY

William B. Tye

Contributions in Economics
and Economic History,
Number 106

GREENWOOD PRESS

New York • Westport, Connecticut • London

Library of Congress Cataloging-in-Publication Data

Tye, W. B. (William B.)
The theory of contestable markets : applications to regulatory and antitrust problems in the rail industry / William B. Tye.
p. cm. — (Contributions in economics and economic history, ISSN 0084–9235 ; no. 106)
Includes bibliographical references.
ISBN 0–313–27337–5 (lib. bdg. : alk. paper)
1. Railroads and state. 2. Competition. 3. Price discrimination. 4. Antitrust law—Economic aspects. I. Title. II. Series.
HE1051.T94 1990
365′.068—dc20 89–25705

British Library Cataloguing in Publication Data is available.

Library of Congress Catalog Card Number: 89–25705
ISBN: 0–313–27337–5
ISSN: 0084–9235

First published in 1990

Greenwood Press, 88 Post Road West, Westport, CT 06881
An imprint of Greenwood Publishing Group, Inc.

Printed in the United States of America

The paper used in this book complies with the Permanent Paper Standard issued by the National Information Standards Organization (Z39.48–1984).

10 9 8 7 6 5 4 3 2 1

To John and Caroline
"Never Drink Your Own Moonshine"

Contents

Preface

This book is a product of many years of work. It hopefully provides the answers to a series of baffling riddles I encountered in my research and consulting practice. I was increasingly asked to evaluate conclusions on major public policy issues involving residual regulation in industries undergoing a transition to deregulation. Many of these applications involved the theory of contestable markets. The theory was offered as a "competitive market model" to guide regulators who, the theory stated, should act as a "surrogate for competition unimpeded by entry barriers." Yet applications almost invariably cited the theory either to justify impediments to contestability or to justify movements away from perfect contestability. Some cynical observers suggested that these efforts simply represent the misuse of the theory by private interests with something to gain in the regulatory process. Others have responded with denial and complete disbelief that the theory would ever be cited for apparently anticompetitive purposes.

The more I explored the theory, the more I became aware that these surprising policy recommendations were founded in the theory itself. Furthermore, they have roots in long-standing disputes over competitive policy for railroads and other regulated industries. For some time, many economists have supported the notion of Ramsey pricing (price discrimination) as the route to welfare gains. Contestability theory also offered the discipline of "hit-and-run entry" as a means of achieving economic efficiency.

But the more closely one examines the theory of contestable markets, the more impossible becomes the task of finding a competitive equilibrium in which Ramsey pricing could be practiced in an environment of perfect contestability. (In the history of economic thought, this dilemma will be recognized as the essence of the historic dispute between Taussig and Pigou over the existence of extreme price discrimination in the rail industry.) This book explains these puzzling policy recommendations as an attempt in practice to reconcile this welfare trade-off in the theory.

The idea of a contradiction between Ramsey pricing and perfect contestability has provoked extreme responses in some economists. For the most part, the economics profession wishes for a world of both unfettered Ramsey pricing and perfect contestability and thus denies that such a trade-off exists. Others respond that the point has been at least implicit in the literature for years. Many others do not understand what the theoretical dispute is all about and assume that it has no practical significance. Finally, a certain number of economists believe that contestability analysis has been discredited or is at least passé.

Experience with applications of these models proves otherwise, however. These applications go further than theoretical demonstrations that Ramsey pricing may require subsidies or other conditions incompatible with perfect contestability. They demonstrate that pricing above marginal cost as required by Ramsey pricing is impossible in every regime of perfect contestability where the two have been offered as the theoretical justification for welfare prescriptions.

And as to the response that the result is obvious, the *Yale Journal on Regulation*, *Regulation*, *Oxford Economic Papers*, and so forth have published numerous papers claiming unqualified success in the application of these theories to actual regulatory problems. Fourteen nationally prominent economists signed a statement of unqualified support for the application of these policies by the Interstate Commerce Commission. Where in this economic literature on applications of contestability are we told that a welfare trade-off is necessary and that movements toward greater contestability are likely to worsen welfare? From reading the prior economic literature on applications of contestability, a practical regulator would hardly conclude that contestability was a virtue akin to the modern notion of virginity—something to be enjoyed via its elimination.

For all the above groups of economists and for the more general reader who has not been exposed to the contestability literature, I include a discussion of both the theoretical and practical aspects of the problem. I also include simple hypothetical numerical examples of the major points throughout the book. I was myself quite startled to see how theoretical issues which almost nobody understood could look ridiculously simple when illustrated with numerical examples.

Some of my friends and referees have told me that I should have written an entirely different book. Instead of writing a book about the application of contestability theory to railroad regulatory issues, perhaps I should have simply written a book on appropriate regulatory policies and theories to be applied to the railroad industry. They complain that I point out the shortcomings of the applications of contestability theory without really providing an integrated set of answers of my own to these regulatory questions. Contrarily, others without direct involvement in railroad regulatory matters are skeptical that a logical body of theories could produce so many paradoxes in practice. Perhaps the reasoning of these applications has not been fully reproduced and understanding them requires a knowledge of "inside baseball." These respondents suggest that I should have written a book about economic theory, where I assume the reader knows nothing about contestability theory or railroad regulation and proceed to develop all of these points via formal models, equations, and theorems. The reader looking for these other books will not find them here, although the interested reader may learn my own views on many of these issues by consulting the bibliography (see, for example, Meyer and Tye 1988).

Instead this is a book somewhere in between theory and application. It starts with certain paradoxes and puzzles which occurred in the application of contestability theory to real problems in the rail industry. Attempts to understand the origins of these puzzles in the theory have led to what I believe are interesting insights into several unsolved conceptual problems in developing appropriate policies for regulatory transitions, including vertical merger theory, vertical foreclosures, and the Pigou-Taussig paradox. This focus means that many of the important issues in the regulatory transition for railroads (such as standards for revenue adequacy, maximum reasonable rates, and market dominance tests) are left for another day. To those who despair that they do not have enough "inside baseball" to understand policy debates and puzzles that motivate the inquiry (or time to go directly to the sources quoted here to judge for themselves), and to the skeptics who believe that these paradoxes simply could not exist, I suggest that you accept them provisionally and see where they lead. The reader with only a passing knowledge of railroad regulation and contestability theory but with patience to pursue some new approaches to old problems will be rewarded with the discovery that contestability theory provides fresh insights into old regulatory and antitrust problems in ways none of us imagined possible.

Some of my critics have taken my identification of the puzzles and paradoxes in these applications as evidence of my entry into what has become a minor industry in the economics profession, "contestability bashing." They complain that perhaps there is nothing wrong with the theory, only its misapplication in practical situations. And many of the ideas that have been incorporated into the contestability approach, such as Ramsey pricing and the Stand-Alone Cost test, actually predate the contestability model.

They question whether the theory and its applications can possibly be as inconsistent as an initial reading of Chapter 1 suggests.

It is certainly true that contestability theory has incorporated prior conceptual developments, but it is not unreasonable to refer to the entire edifice of theory as it was offered in these applications by a single label, just as Marxism incorporates many prior intellectual contributions which Marx synthesized. And some of the applicable concepts of contestability theory in practice present fundamental reconstructions of their theoretical precursors. For example, the Stand-Alone Cost test was initially offered by Alfred Kahn only as a maximum theoretical limit on rates, and Faulhaber's classic article addressed it as a means of protecting the incumbent from uneconomic bypass, not as the only regulatory protection for the captive customer as advanced in applications of contestability theory. Certainly the proponents of the theory in these proceedings believe they are offering an integrated model that provides inclusive guidelines for regulators on every issue at stake in the regulatory transition, and they employ this label. In any event, I use the term "permissive model" with regard to competitive access and vertical merger analysis to indicate the synthesis of the Chicago School and contestability models of antitrust.

Posing the issues as paradoxes arising from the applications of the model is intended only as a pedagogical device to motivate the intellectual odyssey which led me to the conclusions of this book. These puzzlements started with real conflicts among interested parties and with the necessity for regulators to give a clear and consistent explanation of the reasons for their decisions. They are certainly not intended as ad hominem responses to any individuals or groups or to lend support to the notion that contestability analysis is a theory whose time has come and gone.

Circulation of initial drafts of this manuscript has encountered some extreme reactions, including the concern that the pedagogical style conveys a negative overall evaluation of the contributions of contestability theory. On the contrary, contestability theory has provided great insight into major questions that economists have thought to be long settled. It has also improved understanding of numerous issues which had remained unsolved for a considerable time. One of the purposes of this book is to show that these conceptual developments in economic theory provide extremely useful insights into practical problems of accomplishing a successful transition to lesser regulation in many regulated industries. The most profound contributions, however, have not necessarily been the ones anticipated by the original contributors to the theory.

I have found that it is a lot easier in economics to publish a modest or nonexistent contribution to a well-understood problem than to publish an important contribution to a poorly understood problem. The problems addressed in this book are certainly very poorly understood in the economics literature. Whether the contribution is important or not is up to the reader.

In any event, directions for important future research are suggested by these results. The basic problem is that contestability places severe limits on what the potential entrant does for a living while threatening entry. By failing to take the necessary (but unspecified) multimarket conditions into account, one finds that a number of difficulties have arisen in the application of these models. These difficulties in application of the model suggest the necessity to specify the multimarket equilibrium conditions that must be satisfied. Little progress is going to be made in applying the model until these problems are recognized, formalized, and tested.

This book is the product of many discussions over a long period, and I cannot hope to name all who have contributed to my thinking. Nevertheless, to John R. Meyer, Jerry Hausman, Cliff Winston, Jean Tirole, Larry Kolbe, Bill Hogan, George Hall, Mike Scherer, Dutch Leonard, Scott Harvey and many others, special thanks are due for their comments and insights.

1

Introduction

If railroads didn't have any monopolies, you wouldn't have any railroads.

Cunningham (1986)

A series of articles has recently appeared in the economic literature reporting apparently successful efforts to apply the theory of "contestable markets"[1] to practical problems of economic regulation and antitrust enforcement. The new theory has been recently employed as an imprimatur for a remarkable set of recommendations for public policy in industries undergoing a transition to deregulation, most particularly regulated transportation industries. A large number of prominent economists has publicly endorsed the Interstate Commerce Commission's (ICC) acceptance of these recommendations based on contestability theory.[2] Elizabeth E. Bailey and William J. Baumol (1984) report that new policies toward competition during the transition to deregulation are "remarkably consistent" with the teachings of contestability theory. William J. Baumol and Robert D. Willig (1986a) report on "some remarkable decisions in the regulatory and antitrust arenas [that] rely explicitly on the theory of contestability." Baumol and Willig report that "contestability theory can come to the rescue (and several times already has)" in resolving major practical issues of antitrust and regulatory policy in industries undergoing a transition to deregulation. Willig and Baumol (1987) state that "the accomplishments to date [arising from applications of the new theory to railroad regulation] are truly remarkable."

These applications told regulators that they should act as "a surrogate for competition unimpeded by entry barriers" (Baumol and Willig 1983a, 23) and that the theory of contestable markets provides a "competitive market model" for a regime of partially regulated multiproduct firms operating under scale economies and competing directly with one another at prices in excess of marginal costs (Willig and Baumol 1987). The precept guiding these applications was the notion of "a perfectly contestable market, where, under certain entry and exit conditions, the presence of potential competition can generate performance that maximizes market performance" (Morrison and Winston 1987, 54). As initially stated, the task of regulators in the transition to deregulation was to remove impediments to movement toward the new welfare ideal of perfect contestability.

The remainder of this chapter surveys the implementation of the concept of a "surrogate for competition unimpeded by entry barriers" in actual practical applications of the theory. It begins with a brief overview of the critical assumptions and implications of the theory for economic welfare. Of particular interest is the notion that the theory does not predict an unambiguous improvement in welfare arising from movements toward perfect contestability. Conversely, movements away from perfect contestability via impediments to profitable entry ("degradations of contestability") are believed to enhance economic welfare. Readers who are already thoroughly familiar with the regulatory issues that have arisen in the transition to deregulation in the rail industry may wish to skip over the brief survey of the regulatory problems which contestability theory sought to resolve. Finally, each of the major applications of the theory is reviewed and certain puzzles are identified.

An examination of these recent applications of the theory (1) reveals insights into unresolved conceptual problems with the theory of contestable markets, (2) illustrates paradoxes when applying the theory as a "standard of welfare-maximizing structure and behavior" (Baumol 1982, 2; Baumol and Willig 1986a) as regulators seek to act as "surrogates for competition," (3) provides unexpected new understandings of difficult issues in the theory of vertical foreclosures and mergers, and (4) explains puzzling economic policy recommendations that have actually urged movements away from greater contestability to achieve projected welfare gains.

THE RELEVANT THEORY OF PERFECT CONTESTABILITY

The theory of contestable markets states that the threat of entry is equivalent to active competition among incumbents if a market is perfectly contestable. As a market becomes less contestable, the threat of entry becomes less and less credible as a threat to noncompetitive pricing by the incumbent (Schwartz 1986). Perfect contestability via "hit-and-run entry" is achieved if the following principal conditions are satisfied:

1. No barriers to entry: There must be no costs borne by the entrant that are also not borne by the incumbent;
2. No barriers to exit: The entrant can engage in hit-and-run entry because it can exit at no cost, i.e., there are no "sunk costs"; and
3. Assymetric time lags: The time lag in the incumbent's price response to entry must be greater than the time lag in the entrant's ability to exit. As is widely recognized, the key to hit-and-run entry is that the entrant must be able to win "the race between entry and retaliatory measures by incumbents" (Bailey and Baumol 1984, 114). It must be able to enter the market, enjoy profits at prices above competitive levels for a brief period of time, and exit at no cost before the incumbent can retaliate.[3]

Two additional important concepts are that a "feasible contestable industry configuration" requires that each firm be "viable" (total revenues equal or exceed total costs), and that the firm's choice of prices and outputs be "sustainable" (there are no profitable opportunities for hit-and-run entry by an entrant producing any subset of the incumbent's output).[4] Unlike the lagged price response assumed for incumbent firms, perfect information and instantaneous response are assumed to characterize customers' response to such entry.

Very importantly in the theory of contestable markets, potential entrants are able to impose this strong discipline on the incumbent only if they are able to compete on equal terms with no cost or efficiency disadvantages that would impose barriers to entry.[5] The theory of contestability defines "entry barriers" as any cost advantages enjoyed by incumbents but denied to potential entrants.[6] Such entry barriers would afford a "pricing umbrella" for incumbents and allow them to enjoy excess profits because cost disadvantages for the potential entrant would generate immunity to the incumbent from the threat of entry (Willig 1980). Sunk costs qualify as entry barriers under the theory since they are costs to be borne by new entrants but not by incumbents.

The principal developers of the theory of contestability are also the authors of the theory of "multiproduct monopoly." Baumol (1977) has shown that the proper test of a multiproduct monopoly is "subadditivity," the ability of one firm to produce a multitude of products at a lower cost than multiple firms. "Multiproduct economies of scale" can be shown to be a function of "economies of scope"[7] and "product-specific economies of scale" (the tendency of unit attributable costs to decline as volume of a specific product line increases) (Willig 1979b).

The "most dramatic results" of contestability (Bailey 1981) are those of a "contestable monopolist." A firm operating under a regime of "fixed" costs (costs that are invariant to changes in unit of output per time period) but not "sunk" costs (costs that cannot be recouped after exit from a market) would enjoy the security of costless exit and the lowest cost of any potential market structure, but the threat of hit-and-run entry would preclude excess profits. Indeed, since arbitrary subsets of transactions in a perfectly competitive market are contestable markets (Baumol, Panzar, and Willig 1983), it would appear that the chief distinct contribution of the contestability theory would be that of a contestable monopolist.[8]

The theory of contestable markets is offered as a new "standard of welfare-maximizing structure and behavior" (Baumol 1982, 2; Baumol and Willig 1986). More specifically, such markets are said to be characterized by the following welfare properties: (1) no excess profits can be earned; (2) no inefficient firm can survive: (3) no cross subsidies can persist; and (4) predatory pricing must be unprofitable (Baumol 1983a, 42). The last two requirements may provide a fairly permissive constraint on the choice set of prices available to the contestable firm. However, where there are multiple incumbents in a contestable market, sustainable prices must equal marginal cost. Only if the contestable firm is a monopolist is Ramsey pricing above marginal cost sustainable against entry (Baumol 1982).

Critics of the new theory have focused their attention, as is proper when evaluating a new theory that purports to be "no less than a unifying theory as a foundation for the analysis of industrial organization" (Baumol 1982, 15), on the theory itself rather than its application. Because its assumptions on entry and exit seem so implausible, most of the criticisms of the theory have focused on the assumptions required to achieve market forms characterized by hit-and-run entry. Schwartz and Reynolds (1983, 490), for example, characterize these as "grossly unrealistic." Additional evaluation of contestability theory has dwelled on the reasonableness of the entry deterrence and postentry oligopolistic aspects of the assumptions behind hit-and-run entry. (See Spence 1983; Brock 1983, 1062, who refers to "unpalatable hidden assumptions.")

William G. Shepherd (1984, 1986) reviews the theory in the context of the field of industrial organization. He concludes that the theory of "ultra-free entry," to use his preferred terminology, is a polar case without substantial interest as a general theory of market structures, is internally inconsistent, is inconsistent with a vast body of empirical evidence, and is as yet empty of testable hypotheses. Although some would quarrel with his failure to credit the theory's focus on the underrated role of sunk costs in economic theory, Shepherd's contention that the multiproduct monopoly and sustainability analysis is "largely separable" from the contestability theory provides the basis for some interesting insights into applications of the theory to multimarket contestable equilibria (see Chapter 4).

IMPLICATIONS OF CONTESTABILITY THEORY FOR ECONOMIC WELFARE

Contestability theory reopens some of the oldest issues in microeconomics, including ones that are generally thought to be long-settled. Mainstream economic theory assumes a spectrum of competition beginning with Marshall's perfect competitor that prices at marginal cost. At the other end of the spectrum was the (possibly price discriminating) monopolist, which charged prices above marginal costs, associated with Baumol and Bradford (1970), but going back to Ramsey, Boiteux, and Dupuit and others. This monopolist was required to price above marginal cost to achieve firm viability but in the regulated setting was encouraged by regulators to choose the Ramsey optimal price vector. As long as there was a restriction on perfect competition, it was thought that Ramsey pricing would at least minimize the costs imposed by the departure from the world of marginal cost pricing. If there were any proposition in economics upon which economists could be said to agree in this set of models, it was that pricing above marginal cost required a market imperfection of some sort (monopoly, oligopoly, etc.) (Landes and Posner 1981).

Contestability theory has sought to bridge the entire spectrum of the mainstream theory with the notion of a contestable market. Even a firm operating with increasing returns to scale would achieve the least cost industry structure (equivalent to average cost pricing for a single product firm in the old theory), yet be encouraged to charge Ramsey optimal prices above marginal cost by the threat of entry (Baumol, Bailey, and Willig 1977). Ramsey efficient pricing schemes above marginal cost were fully consistent in the new theory with the welfare ideal of perfect contestability. Unlike orthodox theory, contestability theory promised only one welfare standard for all cost structures. With constant returns, the welfare results differed little from the conventional model of perfect competition. With scale economies the welfare standard was the perfectly contestable monopolist practicing Ramsey pricing at prices above marginal costs. Pricing above marginal cost was not viewed in the theory as a sign of imperfect competition, but rather that the optimum industry structure was a monopoly. Market imperfections were defined in terms of barriers to hit-and-run entry, irrespective of scale economies. Contestability (no barriers to hit-and-run entry) did not ordinarily threaten firm viability (equally efficient new entrants would face the same total revenue requirement as the incumbent monopolist) and was not incompatible with Ramsey efficient pricing above marginal costs.

The "Invisible Hand" of Ramsey pricing, admittedly, was said to be "weak" for the contestable monopolist (see Baumol, Bailey, and Willig 1977). In fact, Ramsey prices are only one among the set of sustainable prices generally available to the contestable monopolist (Weiss and Lee 1986). This result is not surprising since the welfare gains from moving to the Ramsey efficient vector of prices within the set of prices sustainable against entry may not be appropriate by an entrant and thus create no incentive for profitable entry. The sustainable monopolist might choose the Ramsey price from the set of sustainable prices, but there was nothing in the theory necessarily forcing it to do so. Nevertheless, choice of the Ramsey optimal price set would offer some protection to the incumbent by eliminating static inefficiencies that might invite entry.

The world of perfect contestability posits a firm that is able to charge a set of prices that recovers total cost in order to be viable, but is constrained to receive total revenue no more than total cost by the threat of entry. Given the assumption of perfect contestability and the requirement for firm viability (no cross subsidy), no welfare gains are possible other than forcing the firm to charge Ramsey prices from among the set of viable and sustainable prices.

These welfare properties of perfectly contestable markets, however, may tell us little regarding the appropriate policy for regulators when confronted with a situation of imperfect contestability. Consider a simple case where the incumbent is protected from entry by a legal monopoly, say the Private Express Statutes prohibiting competitive entry to deliver letter mail in competition with the United States Postal Service. If the goal of regulation is to maximize static economic welfare through a scheme of highly discriminatory Ramsey prices, regulators are instructed by the relevant theory to seek to exploit fully this impediment to contestability in the form of an entry barrier. Highly discriminatory Ramsey prices (Baumol and Bradford 1970) can be shown to minimize the static welfare losses from the necessity to price above marginal cost to recover the revenue requirement. (For applications, see Sherman and George 1979; Tye and Leonard 1983.) Indeed, it is possible to go one step further and observe that degradations of contestability (such as by artificially imposed entry restrictions, cost handicaps to incumbents, and the presence of sunk costs) could be justified by the need to expand the range of sustainable prices available for choice as Ramsey optimal if the set had been restricted by the threat of hit-and-run entry.[9] If the goal of regulators is perceived to be the achievement of economic welfare via static efficient Ramsey prices, the more welcome are such departures from contestability.[10] In practice, the appropriate regulatory strategy would mean exploiting the artificial barrier to entry with extremely high rates for monopoly first-class mail and much lower rates for competitive classes (those subject to competitive entry).

Regulators, however, were simultaneously being told by practitioners of

Table 1–1
Revenue/Variable Cost Proposals for Postal Rates of Selected Competitive Classes of Mail

	MCCM*	Ramsey Price
Parcel Post	130	117
Priority Mail	210	123
Express Mail	221	122

* Maximum Competitive Contribution Methodology.

Source: MCCM is found in Direct Testimony of George R. Hall, before the Postal Rate Commission, filed 27 October 1987, Docket No. R87-1; Ramsey Price is found in Direct Testimony of Frank A Scott, Jr., filed 14 September 1987, in the same proceeding.

contestability analysis to act as "surrogates for competition unimpeded by entry barriers." This would mean setting postal prices as *if* the Postal Service faced the threat of entry for first-class mail. (In effect, elasticities and rates for first-class mail would be computed in the Ramsey model as if the Postal Service faced the threat of entry.) First-class rates would be sharply lower than Ramsey levels and competitive classes would be set at net revenue maximizing levels (Allen 1986), not the much lower levels indicated by the Ramsey model.

This welfare dilemma in the theory of contestable markets translates directly into a practical problem for regulators. As shown in Table 1–1, forcing the Postal Service to price as if its protected monopoly of first class mail did not exist would produce the rate proposals in column 1, labelled the "maximum competitive contribution methodology" (MCCM). Under MCCM, the Postal Service would maximize the net revenue contributions of competitive classes and minimize the contributions from monopoly classes. Ramsey pricing, as shown in column 2, would exploit the monopoly to reduce rates of competitive classes to much lower levels.

In such practical applications of the theory where markets are imperfectly contestable, the theory of perfect contestability does not give clear instructions to regulators. Should they price as if the market were perfectly contestable or exploit departures from perfect contestability via Ramsey pricing? Unlike in the world of perfect contestability, regulators and antitrust authorities seeking guidance from contestability theory must first decide what end of the conventional spectrum of cost structures they are dealing with in answering this question. Where production technology is subject to constant returns, prices will equal marginal costs and movements towards perfect contestability would appear to be unambiguously welfare-enhancing. Removing impediments to contestability would promise *X*-efficiency (Leibenstein 1966) benefits and pricing efficiencies would not possibly be sacrificed. This welfare prescription is, of course, subject to (1) the pathological cases of unsustainability of the Faulhaber (1975) variety, (2) the usual "second best" caveats of conventional economic theory, and (3) concerns expressed by Schwartz and Reynolds (1983), Schwartz (1986), Stiglitz (1987), and Dasgupta and Stiglitz (1988) that small departures from perfect contestability may produce large departures from the optimum welfare properties of the model. But this, of course, is more or less what the conventional theory would tell us.

Such reasonably clear welfare prescriptions no longer exist once one considers an imperfectly contestable monopolist operating in a regime of increasing returns to scale. There, one enters the uncertain world of welfare trade-offs, where movements toward perfect contestability promise to achieve the discipline of the threat of entry but may also deprive incumbents of more Ramsey efficient prices that are available only because of departures from perfect contestability. Regulators are then asked by the theory to choose between enhancing Ramsey pricing and advancing contestability. Indeed, they may fear, and certainly will be told by the firms they are seeking to guide through a successful transition to deregulation, that removing impediments to contestability (or equivalently forcing the regulated firm to operate as if they did not exist) will eliminate *any* set of prices that will make the firm viable, in addition to foreclosing ones with superior Ramsey efficient properties.

Recognition of a perceived welfare trade-off between (1) the static welfare gains from Ramsey pricing (and in the most extreme case the ability to achieve a sustainable equilibrium at all) and (2) the *X*-efficiency (Leibenstein 1966) properties of the discipline of hit-and-run entry thus becomes an insight for understanding many puzzling policy prescriptions that have emerged in these recent applications of the theory (Tye 1987e; Anderson and Rennicke 1987). Before illustrating this welfare trade-off in each of the major applications, the next section provides an overview of the regulatory issues that the theory sought to address in the rail industry.

REGULATORY AND ANTITRUST ISSUES IN THE TRANSITION TO DEREGULATION IN THE RAIL INDUSTRY

Applications of the theory of contestable markets have not been confined to the airline industry (Bailey and Panzar 1981). In fact, conditions for effective contestability have been purported to exist in industries ranging from airline computerized reservation systems (Baumol 1983c) to the railroad industry (Baumol 1984b).

A series of applications of the theory to regulatory and antitrust problems in the rail industry are particularly revealing. Regulatory reform in the rail industry has required a fundamental reappraisal of virtually every traditional regulatory institution. As such, it calls for entirely new ways of thinking and provides an ideal climate for assessing the feasibility of applying new theories of industrial organization such as the theory of contestable markets.

Other published works have addressed the elements of regulatory reform in the rail industry in greater detail (Keeler 1983; Friedlaender and Spady 1981) and should be consulted by the reader unfamiliar with the history of railroad economic regulation and the provisions of the Staggers Rail Act that changed fundamentally a century of regulatory precedent.

The essence of the regulatory transition problem in the rail industry may be readily summarized. (See Meyer and Tye 1988, for details.) The rail industry is subject to substantial sunk costs since assets are long-lived and specific to certain geographic markets. Much of the traffic is subject to effective competition from competing railroads, other modes, competing origins and destinations, or competing products. Some shippers, however, ship commodities for which rail has a substantial competitive advantage over alternative modes. Further, these shippers have sunk considerable costs in specific locations or signed contracts which make them captive to individual railroads. The difficult problem in the transition is to permit maximum leeway for competitive forces while maintaining the regulatory protection that was relied upon by captive shippers when they sank costs in facilities based on the presumption of continued regulation and the unavailability of the usual contractual protections against "opportunistic behavior" in such circumstances.

To understand how contestability theory affected the thinking of the ICC on appropriate policies of regulatory reform to address this problem, it is useful to divide the issues of rail regulatory reform into six major concerns:

1. Balancing the conflicting goals of the regulatory transition;
2. Standards for revenue adequacy;
3. Standards for cooperation among competitors (competitive access);

4. Standards for maximum reasonable rates;
5. Standards for determining ''market dominance,'' a condition necessary for the Commission to assert jurisdiction over rates; and
6. Standards for granting antitrust immunity to mergers.

Balancing the Conflicting Goals of the Regulatory Transition

The Staggers Rail Act was a compromise between shipper and carrier interests designed to balance four potentially competing legislative goals: (1) "revenue adequacy" for the carriers; (2) regulatory protection for "captive" (or "market dominant") shippers for whom competitive markets were deemed not to be available as a guarantee of a "reasonable rate" because of "the absence of effective competition"; (3) relaxed regulatory constraints for competitive traffic; and (4) incentives for revenue enhancement of deficit traffic. The history of railroad regulatory policy before and after Staggers may be largely summed up as an attempt to resolve these conflicting objectives (Tye 1983). Shipper interests believed they had granted major concessions to deregulate competitive traffic (goal 3) and to achieve revenue adequacy (goal 1), while receiving in return residual regulation to protect captive shippers (goal 1) and guarantees that captive shippers would not be required to fund losses for certain categories of competitive traffic (goal 4).

Shortly after passage of the Staggers Act, the ICC began a series of decisions that many shippers believed to have eviscerated the guarantees supposedly incorporated in the legislation. These decisions, many of which were founded on the theories of Ramsey pricing and contestable markets, were alarming for two major reasons: (1) they had the consequence of undermining the competition that was the initial rationale for deregulation, and (2) they threatened a successful transition to deregulation by encouraging reform (or "tinkering" depending on your point of view) of the Staggers Act through legislative intervention (Meyer and Tye 1988).

As discussed further below, the intersection of the Commission's new market dominance standards and its rate reasonableness standards produced a "catch–22" for the captive shipper. This dilemma arose because a shipper first had to prove the existence of the "lack of effective competition" in a market dominance proceeding before the Commission would conduct a proceeding to determine rate reasonableness. But according to the theory of Ramsey pricing, the lesser the level of effective competition, the higher would be the recommended Ramsey rate. Shippers rightly wondered how any consistent body of economic theory could produce such perverse results.

Standards for Revenue Adequacy

Shippers' fears of regulatory misconstruction of the legislative compromises of the Staggers Rail Act were heightened by a series of ICC decisions that greatly modified prior standards of revenue needs for railroads. Relying on the theory of contestable markets, the Commission rejected the traditional utility rate base/rate of return standard which employed depreciated original cost. While ultimately shrinking from defining the investment base as the cost of a brand new entrant, the Commission nevertheless employed a "current cost" standard that, together with the Stand-Alone Cost (SAC) test (1984e), ensured that virtually every railroad was declared revenue inadequate and every rate reasonable (Tye 1986d). Furthermore, contestability theory was invoked to justify the elevation of achievement of revenue adequacy as the highest goal of regulators. According to the theory, all the rest mentioned in the Staggers Act should be subordinated to that goal. Incredulous members of Congress wondered how railroads found to be grossly revenue inadequate and without any captive traffic were nevertheless able to acquire pipelines and shipping companies. The ICC ultimately revised its revenue adequacy test to the traditional depreciated original cost standard, perhaps in response to these concerns.

Standards for Cooperation among Competitors (Competitive Access)

Railroads are a network industry characterized by a large degree of cooperation among carriers. Within "switching districts" carriers may jointly own a local company that switches cars among the facilities of several line-haul carriers serving the same city, or carriers may provide "reciprocal switching" for one another. Movements from origin to destination frequently require service by more than one railroad, and competition between railroads may be present for only a part of the total movement because one carrier or another controls access to either the origin or the destination. Prior to the Staggers Act, tariffs were often "open-routed" in the sense that almost any available carrier could offer to serve the traffic. "Joint rates" from origin to destination were established under antitrust immunity in multilateral rate bureaus. Any cancellations of these joint rates and through routes were subject to suspension and investigation by the ICC.

In response to complaints that the prior system encouraged inefficient circuitous routing of traffic, the Staggers Act greatly expanded a carrier's right to refuse to interline or provide switching services to competing carriers. The ICC relied on a variant of the theory of contestable markets and these legislative changes to permit railroads to cancel intercarrier cooperative agreements on a grand scale. The effect of this permissive approach to cancellations of competitive access was to curb significantly the scope of intramodal competition, as few shippers had the benefit of rail-to-rail competition from origin to destination. Many shippers feared that the ICC was placing its imprimatur on the elimination of the intramodal competition that had been the rationale for deregulation.

Standards for Maximum Reasonable Rates

Railroad interests initially propounded as a test of rate reasonableness that railroads be allowed to practice Ramsey pricing, a variant of value-of-service ratemaking that goes back considerably in the history of railroading. According to the theory, railroads would "charge what the market will bear." The rationale was grounded in the theoretical literature predating contestability analysis, which stated that the economic costs of pricing above marginal costs to achieve revenue adequacy could be minimized via such price discrimination.

Shippers retorted that Ramsey pricing would assign the highest rates to the most price inelastic demands, that is, those most subject to market dominance and thereby supposedly qualifying for regulatory protection under Staggers. While not directly conceding this "catch–22" problem, the Commission rejected Ramsey pricing as infeasible and seized upon another standard which was initially proposed only as an afterthought to Ramsey pricing—the Stand-Alone Cost (SAC) test. According to the SAC test, a maximum reasonable rate would never exceed the level which a stand-alone shipper could provide the service for itself. Although the SAC test had actually predated contestability analysis (Faulhaber 1975) as a test to protect a monopolist from uneconomic entry, it was later deemed by applications of contestability theory to be the only appropriate cost-based constraint on Ramsey pricing. Many shippers rejected the test in practice as a thinly disguised effort to eliminate any effective constraint on rates of captive shippers as envisaged by the Staggers Act (Tye 1985b, 1986a).

Standards for Market Dominance

Prior to the Staggers Act the ICC had used four tests to determine market dominance:

1. Cost test: An examination of the revenue/variable cost of the traffic at issue;
2. Market share test: An examination of the market share of the carrier(s);
3. Substantial investment/long-term contracts: An examination of sunk costs and contractual restrictions on shipper choices; and

4. Rate bureau test: Whether the rate had been established collusively by the carriers under antitrust immunity according to a rate bureau agreement.

These standards were replaced by "evidentiary guidelines" (Tye 1983):

1. Intramodal competition: An examination of competition among railroads for the traffic at issue;
2. Intermodal competition: An examination of competition from other modes;
3. Geographic competition: An examination of competition from substitute origins or destinations; and
4. Product competition: An examination of competition from substitute products.

Railroad interests asserted that the new standards supported their conclusion that the revenue/variable cost ratio was an irrelevant measure of market dominance. These assertions further heightened concerns that shippers faced a "catch–22." Captive traffic tended to have the highest revenue/variable cost ratios. These high ratios were claimed to be irrelevant to market dominance proceedings but rather evidence of efficient Ramsey prices for market dominant traffic (Tye 1984a, 1984b). Shippers were understandably skeptical of such theories, which once again had the practical effect of eliminating virtually any regulatory constraint on rates for captive shippers.

Merger Policies

Soon after passage of the Staggers Act came a series of proposed intramodal railroad mergers and proposed intermodal rail-water carrier mergers. The ICC initially took a very permissive approach to possible anticompetitive consequences of these proposals, citing the essence of contestability theory (Baumol and Willig 1983a, 1983b; Willig and Baumol 1987; Baumol 1979, 1984a, 1984b) and the newly unleashed forces of competition as sufficient competitive safeguards. But as with the permissive policy towards foreclosures of competitive access discussed above, critics complained that the ICC was approving the elimination of the very competition that was the rationale for regulatory reform. The permissive approach nevertheless became effective policy until the contradictions became impossible to ignore in the proposed merger of the Santa Fe and Southern Pacific railroads (Tye 1987e). The commissioner who led the opposition to the merger at the ICC cited numerous contradictions in the applicants' reliance on economic theory in his decision to reject the application. Many observers thought it odd indeed that contestability theory was cited as support for the merger on the grounds that excessive competition was driving prices to levels inconsistent with the Commission's revenue adequacy standards. Further, contestability theory was cited in opposition to remedial measures that would restore the competition that would be eliminated by a proposed merger (Tye 1986b).

Role of the Theory of Contestable Markets in Rail Regulatory Reform

The theory of contestable markets can thus be seen to provide an answer to each of the major policy concerns in the transition to deregulation in the rail industry. Some of these conclusions provided results which were highly disturbing to captive shippers who believed that the compromises that were critical to the passage of the Staggers Act were slighted in both the theory and the Commission's decisions.

The pages that follow do not attempt to solve all of these issues of regulatory reform in the rail industry. Rather, the purpose is to gain more general insights into the theory of contestable markets which will also be useful in a broad range of applications outside the rail industry. To do so, we must address in more detail certain paradoxes and inconsistencies that have arisen in the following applications of the theory:

1. The use of contestability theory to evaluate the potential anticompetitive effects of intramodal railroad mergers and intermodal rail/water carrier mergers;
2. The proposed use of the Stand-Alone Cost (SAC) test as the only economically appropriate constraint on rates for a captive rail shipper under ICC rate regulation;
3. The assertion that revenue/marginal cost ratios are misleading indicators of "market dominance," a condition that the ICC must find in the relevant market prior to assuming jurisdiction over the reasonableness of a particular rail rate;
4. Advice to regulators both that they should and should not promote contestability in industries undergoing a transition to deregulation by granting new entrants "competitive access" to "bottleneck" sunk facilities of incumbents; and
5. Predictions of market structure and performance in a deregulated airline industry also provide additional insights into applications of the theory.

RECENT APPLICATIONS OF THE THEORY OF CONTESTABLE MARKETS

Merger Analysis

The theory of contestable markets has been invoked (Baumol 1983a, 1986a) to recommend a proposed intermodal vertical merger between a rail carrier and a water carrier that would create benefits not otherwise achievable. According to applications of the theory, a merger of a noncontestable railroad with a barge line operating over allegedly highly contestable routes could never degrade the contestability (i.e., cause a violation of one of the necessary conditions for contestability) of the water routes affected by the merger. Thus it is asserted that there need be no fear of anticompetitive behavior of the vertically merged rail-barge entity against independent water carriers who must interchange traffic with the merged water carrier/railroad to compete in the relevant markets.

But a puzzling paradox emerges between the theory of contestability as the answer to possible postmerger anticompetitive behavior and the particular claims of significant merger benefits advanced in these merger proceedings. The logical difficulty is as follows. Demonstrating meaningful merger benefits in the form of the particular claimed efficiency gains requires the existence of premerger market imperfections that could be eliminated by the proposed merger, and only by the merger. The ability to achieve *the particular benefits* claimed in these proceedings is, however, at variance with the assumption of a highly contestable market prior to the merger. To demonstrate the absence of any possible postmerger anticompetitive impacts, contestability theory is cited by merger proponents to demonstrate that these same market imperfections were de minimis, both before and after the merger. Merger advocates applying contestability theory to justify antitrust immunity to these vertical mergers have never figured out a way of solving both problems simultaneously and they switch from the assumptions of incontestable to highly contestable as required.

The logical difficulty is illustrated most clearly when it is asserted (Baumol 1983a) that vertical integration of railroads and barge carriers would provide significant benefits of "pricing coordination" by eliminating inefficient overcharging arising from end-to-end connecting carriers charging separate "proportional rates" while facing downward-sloping demand functions (Baumol 1983b, 1986a). The barge industry was also said to be virtually perfectly contestable, that contestability in the barge industry could not be affected by vertical integration, that there could be no increase in monopoly profit by a monopolist integrating vertically into a perfectly contestable market, and that efficiencies of pricing coordination could be accomplished only through vertical integration.

But the existence of near perfect contestability in the relevant water routes would rule out the particular market imperfections in pricing that were the alleged sources of the merger benefits. (See Tye 1984c, and agreement by Baumol 1984a.) By the same token, support for vast rail mergers and intermodal mergers on the grounds of eliminating inefficient overcharging by end-to-end rail carriers with power over price (Baumol 1984b) was inconsistent with the assertion (Baumol 1984b) that the rail industry was effectively contestable. The allegation that such mergers eliminated inefficient pricing practices was also at variance with the assertion (Baumol and Willig 1983a, 1983b) that unconstrained rail carriers would unilaterally set Ramsey-efficient prices without benefit of regulatory guidance in an industry in which a majority of the traffic moved interline (Tye 1984c).

Although less obvious, the types of "transactions costs"[11] that were claimed to be reduced by these proposed mergers were likely to be de minimis in a contestable market precisely because the strong assumptions of contestability protected buyers and sellers fully from "opportunistic behavior" in the barge industry (Klein, Crawford, and Alchian 1978) without the need for contracts. Conversely, if such benefits are achievable only through vertical merger, contestability on the affected water routes will necessarily be degraded. According to the theory of multiproduct monopoly, the stronger are the economies of scope,[12] the more likely is the incumbent to be invulnerable to the threat of competitive entry by a specialized competitor offering only a single product or service. The "contest" in a contestable market must take place at a scale and scope sufficient for the entrant to suffer no cost disadvantages relative to the incumbent; that is, there must be no barriers to entry.[13]

The alleged transactions costs efficiency gains resulting only from such vertical mergers, if present, would meet the definition of economies of scope and would constitute what the theory of contestability defines as an "economies of scope entry barrier"[14] when, as they claim, they are available only to a merged entity and therefore denied to stand-alone rivals. The existence of specialized potential entrants with higher transactions costs than vertically integrated incumbents would violate the assumption that there be "no cost discrimination against entrants," and contestability would be necessarily degraded. Where a railroad was not subject to the restraints of contestability in the coal fields, vertical integration of a railroad and a barge line would, under these conditions, necessarily degrade the purported near-perfect contestability of the barge industry for the relevant vertically related markets (Tye 1985a).

The Stand-Alone Cost Test

A similar logical difficulty also affects another regulatory progeny of contestability theory, the Stand-Alone Cost (SAC) test for a maximum reasonable rail rate for captive coal traffic. To protect captive shippers (i.e., those subject to market dominance[15]), the specialized SAC ceiling[16] is offered to regulators as the only necessary guide for maximum rates. The rationale offered was that the SAC test is a sufficient condition for an equilibrium market price in a perfectly contestable market. Carriers, meanwhile, were advised to employ Ramsey pricing, with prices substantially in excess of marginal costs, on the grounds that substantial economies of scale and scope in the rail industry required such prices in order to be "revenue adequate," a term of art in rail rate regulation equivalent, at least in concept, to firm viability in contestability.

However, the specialized SAC test is not a necessary and sufficient "surrogate for contestability" in an industry composed of multiproduct firms enjoying economies of scope (Weiss and Lee 1986). The reasons for this should be clear from the above discussion. Under the hypothesized cost structure of substantial economies of scale and scope, the market price for each product in a contestable market will not be determined uniquely by the costs of a specialized entrant pricing to recover its SAC. Economies of scope ordinarily imply that a specialized producer cannot survive in competition with a full-line competitor (Baumol, Panzar, and Willig 1982, 247). The market price for each product will ordinarily be below the SAC price ceiling, and the SAC price will only be a limit on the theoretical maximum price even under conditions of a perfectly contestable market.

Proponents have suggested that the solution is to extend all the benefits of economies of scale and scope to the surrogate for competition in order to circumvent this difficulty via so-called "group stand-alone costs." But this approach imposes on the potential entrant the cost structure of the incumbent, thus taking us full circle back to the original problem of allocating joint cost.[17] Meyer and Tye (1985) also point out that the SAC test ironically ignored the role of *buyers' sunk costs* in establishing a surrogate, even though they (1) were explicitly considered in the relevant legislation governing rail rates during the transition to deregulation, (2) are crucial determinants in establishing that the shipper is "captive" and thus deserving of regulatory protection under the relevant legislation, (3) are recognized by the theory as the key determinant of market structure when found on the sellers' side, and (4) impose the necessary restrictions on buyers' choices that are believed needed to achieve revenue adequacy via extreme price discrimination (Meyer and Tye 1988).

Applications to Issues of Competitive Access

The theory of contestable markets was initially cited to support the idea that regulators should foster contestability by reducing the importance of sunk costs in industries undergoing a transition to deregulation. "Rather than relying exclusively on traditional rate and entry regulation," the preferred policy is "government intervention to insure equal access to the sunk facility" (Bailey and Baumol 1984, 124). Bailey (1981) recommended consideration of the use of trackage rights (regulatory enforced access by one carrier to another's right-of-way to eliminate the role of sunk costs in preventing contestability) in the rail industry to reduce the need for regulatory review of rate reasonableness. Researchers who have accepted the characterization of perfect contestability as the welfare optimum have generally supported such "competitive access" as a means of eliminating barriers to contestability if such markets are found to be imperfectly contestable (Morrison and Winston 1987, 55).

More recently, however, applications of the theory have characterized promotion of "competitive access" via trackage rights to reinstitute competition eliminated as a consequence of a rail merger as the "worst possible remedy that a malevolent mind could devise" (Baumol 1984b). The basis in contestability theory for this change in recommendation of policy toward competitive access has not yet been fully explained. While objections to specific policies for determining the price of access have been raised, more generic concerns apparently motivate the objections to regulatory intervention to enhance contestability via competitive access policies in industries undergoing a transition to deregulation. These concerns apparently arise from beliefs that promotion of contestability can actually lead to welfare losses by depriving the incumbent firm of the ability to achieve a viable natural monopoly by exploiting the existence of sunk costs to further the price discrimination via Ramsey pricing believed necessary for revenue adequacy (Baumol 1985a).

But (1) the claim that maintenance or enhancement of direct competition among incumbents has adverse effects on economic welfare because it drives prices to marginal costs and deprives firms of the marginal power they need to practice Ramsey pricing (Baumol and Willig 1985a, 1985b, 1985c; Baumol 1985b) is incongruent with (2) the "competitive market model" offered in market dominance proceedings, that is, contentions that an equilibrium of revenue-adequate firms operating under multiproduct scale economies (prices exceed marginal costs) and competing directly in the same markets (the mutton and wool analogy discussed below) is a viable and sustainable contestable equilibrium. This incongruence shows up most clearly in applications of contestability to market dominance determinations, to which we turn.

Use of Revenue/Variable Costs Ratios in Market Dominance Determination

The theory of contestable markets has been used to assess whether a rail firm has market dominance over a particular traffic movement (the ICC must find market dominance if it is to assert jurisdiction over the reasonableness of the rate). One such index of market dominance that has been offered is the ratio of revenue/marginal cost, as approximated by the revenue/variable cost ratio (Tye 1984a).

The theory of contestability has been invoked to conclude that high revenue/marginal cost ratios are misleading indicators of market dominance for multiproduct firms. The offered counterexample is mutton and wool multiproduct firms operating in a contestable industry composed of many shepherds who must charge in excess of the marginal costs of mutton and wool to recover joint costs and be "revenue adequate." (See Willig 1984a; Baumol and Willig 1985a, 11, for the hypothetical example.) As with railroads, the proposed counterexample assumes that the products are not produced in fixed proportions. The proposed counterexample maintains that to recover total costs, prices must be in excess of marginal costs and must be sustainable against intense price competition among multiproduct incumbents and the threat of entry in a contestable market. The model that is offered as a guide to regulators when they act as a surrogate for competition is contestability among multiproduct firms operating under scale economies and charging Ramsey prices above marginal costs in the same market as required for revenue adequacy (firm viability).

This model of contestable competitors practicing Ramsey pricing directly contravenes Baumol, Panzar, and Willig's demonstration (1982, 245, 317; 1986; Baumol 1982, 2, 5) that price must equal marginal cost in a contestable market to achieve sustainability (i.e., absence of opportunities for profitable entry), unless the market is occupied by a natural monopolist. But marginal cost pricing by multiple incumbents as required to achieve sustainability against profitable entry in a perfectly contestable market means that Ramsey prices in excess of marginal cost are no longer possible, and the firms become nonviable (cannot recover total costs). The firm viability and sustainability requirements in this model offered to regulators appear to be in direct contradiction in a world of perfect contestability.

The contradiction between the firm viability and sustainability requirements in a regime of multiple contestable incumbents charging Ramsey prices may be best illustrated by reference to the actual numbers offered in the supposed counterexample of shepherds. In the hypothetical example, the lamb costs $10 to raise, and incremental costs of wool and mutton are $1 and $2, respectively. The SAC of wool is $11 and the SAC of mutton is $12. Ramsey prices are assumed equal to $7 for wool and $6 for mutton. By hypothesis, prices exceed marginal costs in the supposed counterexample.

The Ramsey prices of $6 and $7 satisfy the firm viability test and the SAC test, but they violate the sustainability-against-entry requirement. Since these Ramsey prices exceed marginal costs by assumption, a new entrant can profitably expand output of mutton and wool at incremental costs less than the respective Ramsey prices and use some of the additional profit from additional output to successfully contest the entire output of an incumbent. If the ratio of price to marginal cost is approximated by the revenue/variable cost ratio, shepherds will earn $7 and $3.50 for every incremental dollar spent grooming and feeding the animals, respectively. Put another way, output of mutton and wool from an individual sheep is indeterminate as long as Ramsey pricing above marginal costs is employed by any of the numerous contestable incumbents. They all can profitably expand output and sell into a perfectly elastic demand as long as prices exceed marginal costs.

The fundamental contradiction between Ramsey pricing (where prices exceed marginal costs) and perfect contestability among incumbents (where prices charged by multiple incumbents must equal marginal costs and Ramsey pricing is infeasible) is not a mere theoretical curiosity. Baumol and Willig (1983b, 36–37) apply the model to assert that Ramsey pricing principles are applicable to a regime of railroads engaging in intramodal competition with one another. The paradox is that the equilibrium would be viable and sustainable only because of departures from perfect contestability. (In the above example, multiple shepherds could be assumed to achieve sustainable prices in excess of marginal costs via collusion or oligopolistic interactions.) A successful movement to perfect contestability would force firms to charge prices equal to marginal cost and prevent firm viability. (Equilibrium could only be established in shepherding with Ramsey prices via a monopoly or by reintroducing the departures from perfect contestability.) If one believes that Ramsey pricing is essential to firm viability in a deregulated equilibrium, the conflict between Ramsey pricing and perfect contestability has significant implications for regulatory policy towards promoting competition during a transition to deregulation.

Predictions of the Effects of Airline Deregulation

The market for air travel between two cities was originally cited as a good example of a contestable market. In support of airline deregulation, Bailey and Panzar (1981) predicted that contestability on individual airline routes would suffice to produce the competitive result even when the incumbents were few. However, more recent evidence by Graham, Kaplan, and Sibley (1983), Bailey, Graham, and Kaplan (1985), Morrison and Winston (1986, 1987), Call and Keeler (1985), and Levine (1987) suggests disturbing departures from the results predicted by contestability analysis in airline markets. Bailey and Baumol (1984, 130) state that "this evidence suggests that the contestability benchmark does not fully hold sway in the first five years after deregulation." Significantly, to explain the departures they invoke the presence of factors observed only at the level of the firm or the entire domestic industry and not at the level of a purportedly contestable individual route—excess capacity, labor contracts, and network effects (economies of scope among routes).

IMPLICATIONS OF RECENT APPLICATIONS OF CONTESTABILITY

Do the logical difficulties, surprising policy recommendations, and paradoxes in recent applications of contestability theory have underlying causes, or are the problems simply empirical ones encountered in a practical effort to apply a logically coherent body of theory? Both would seem to be true to some degree.

A common logical problem in the applications of contestability theory to merger analysis and the Stand-Alone Cost test is readily apparent. There can be "no cost discrimination against entrants" (Baumol 1982) in contestable markets, but both these applications of contestability theory explicitly assume cost disadvantages to the entrant. Indeed, the existence or creation of such cost disadvantages was the point of the exercise. Presumably, there would be no efficiency rationale for the proposed vertical merger or the need for a SAC constraint on Ramsey prices if there were not significant economies of scope. In the case of the application to vertical mergers, the proposed merger itself was alleged to create the cost disadvantages to entrants. In the case of the proposed Stand-Alone Cost test, cost disadvantages to entrants arose from economies of scale and scope which necessitated the need for Ramsey pricing and the recommendation of the SAC test to constrain Ramsey pricing via a surrogate for competition.[18]

The recent problematic applications of the theory to vertical mergers and the Stand-Alone Cost test thus have a theme in common: the application of the theory of contestable markets at the level of a highly specialized entrant while failing to give equal weight to the significance assigned to the theory of multiproduct monopoly and in particular economy of scope entry barriers in determining the cost-minimizing market structure.[19] The potential entrant suffers a cost disadvantage by definition of the joint-cost allocation problem if it enters only at the level of the specialized SAC entrant. More formally, the SAC test is not a necessary and sufficient test for a sustainable multiproduct monopoly (Weiss and Lee 1986) and thus is not a "surrogate for contestability."[20] The presence of economies of scope and scale in the SAC applications thus forces the potential entrant to achieve a scale of output or range of services (group Stand-Alone Cost) where the original cost allocation problem reasserts itself.

A common response to the above logical difficulties of applying contestability theory to vertical mergers and the SAC test is to disbelieve that such a logically integrated body of theory such as contestable markets could actually produce such odd results in practical applications of the theory. Perhaps the applications of the theory have been misrepresented or practitioners of the theory have been misinterpreted. Or perhaps the logical difficulties in the applications can be tidied up simply by dropping inconsistent claims for the theory (Tye 1987e).

To some degree, logical difficulties arising from internally inconsistent claims can be corrected simply by consistently applying the theory itself. The specific claims of pricing efficiencies or reduced transactions costs could be dropped in vertical merger analysis, the claims of merger benefits could perhaps be crafted so that they did not violate the strong assumptions of contestability, or a necessary reduction in the degree of contestability in the affected markets as a consequence of the proposed vertical merger could be conceded. In the case of the SAC test, it should be noted that the test is only a necessary but not sufficient property of a surrogate for competition in the circumstances where it has been offered, and we must continue to search for additional, more constraining tests.[21]

However, the logical difficulties of competitive access issues are not so easily resolved, because they run through the mainstream of vertical foreclosure theory. Applications of contestability theory make assumptions where the ambivalence of the entire literature on vertical foreclosure (see Warren-Boulton 1978, for example) may be seen with clarity. This literature is filled with the claims that restrictive vertical market practices have substantial potential for efficiency gains, while other writers caution that antitrust authorities must be vigilant to prevent reductions in competition.[22] The strong implication is that it is possible to have one without the other. While the literature often embraces one or the other extreme explanation, contestability theory provides the idealized market environment where the two claimed results of vertical market restrictions may arise from the very same types of market imperfections. Indeed, a highly interesting result of applying contestability to problems of vertical foreclosure is the conclusion that achievement of the claimed efficiency gains from vertical foreclosures requires degradations of contestability.[23]

Chapter 2 discusses in more detail this common feature of these applications. Here, the theory of contestable markets has been offered in support of granting antitrust immunity to vertical mergers where one of the merging firms operates in highly contestable markets prior to the proposed merger and another possesses market power. The results show that the assumption of a high degree of contestability in one market prior to a proposed vertical merger places extreme limits on the kinds of efficiency gains that are achievable by a proposed merger. In particular, the specific claims of meaningful pricing efficiencies and reduced transactions costs arising from recent proposed vertical mergers are at variance with the optimal welfare properties of highly contestable markets. Conversely, meaningful efficiency gains consistent with the optimal welfare properties of the premerger markets may result and may do so only via the proposed merger. Here, contestability will be necessarily degraded (potential entrants will suffer efficiency disadvantages) in mergers where one of the merger partners possesses market power. Further, the resulting degradation of contestability necessarily precludes the "efficiency" defense for postmerger vertical foreclosures ("refusals to deal") by the merged firm. These findings have considerable significance for the entire debate over vertical foreclosure theory, because the permissive theory relies heavily on the need for market foreclosure to achieve efficiency gains.

The results of Chapter 2 raise further paradoxes about the theories of vertical foreclosure commonly cited to condone restrictive vertical practices and potentially anticompetitive vertical mergers. Chapter 3 attempts to resolve them by examining recent examples where the theory of contestable markets has been used to justify permissive attitudes by regulators and the courts toward denials of competitive access (vertical foreclosures) in the rail industry. Puzzling discrepancies between the theory's predictions and fact in the rail industry are shown to arise from the existence of substantial transactions, information, and sunk costs, the presence of which fundamentally alters the conclusions of the widely accepted permissive model of vertical foreclosures. A pricing rule for opening up competitive access is proposed for the rail industry, and some of the objections to it are considered. The results could offer an important new approach to resolving other debates over vertical restraints generally.

A common thread in the logical difficulties in the market dominance, competitive access, and airline deregulation applications is not so obvious, but Chapter 4 will show that they too share a common problem. As noted above, the theory of contestable markets promises unique results where the multiproduct monopolist operates in a regime of fixed but not sunk costs. The potential entrants in the theory "spring from the head of Zeus," and no particular assumptions are made regarding existing employment of the necessary resources available to the entrant while awaiting the opportunity for profitable entry (other than the implicit assumption that exit from the current employment is costless). So far, the theory is ceteris paribus and thus implicitly assumes that the necessary multimaket equilibrium among contestable incumbents and contestable entrants is sustainable against entry and viable for each of the firms.

The last three applications of the theory, however, make highly specific assumptions regarding what firms in the "pool of potential entrants" (Bailey and Baumol 1984) are doing for a living while threatening entry—they are assumed to be engaging in direct intramodal competition with the incumbent while practicing Ramsey pricing at prices in excess of marginal costs. But these specific assumptions regarding the competitive relationships between potential entrants and incumbents will be shown to be inconsistent with a sustainable and viable contestable multimarket equilibrium. Chapter 4 shows that firms charging such Ramsey prices are vulnerable to profitable hit-and-run entry when the handicap of the assumed lagged price responses of incumbents is explicitly taken into account. The extreme difficulties encountered in establishing the multimarket conditions necessary for Ramsey prices that are sustainable against profitable entry raise major questions as to how the theory would serve as a "surrogate for competition" by regulators.

The perception of major viability and sustainability problems in markets approaching perfect contestability is not simply a theoretical curiosity. This perception, in turn, leads applications of contestability theory to conclude that one must impose (1) specific restrictions on consumer choice (demand substitution between the offerings of the potential entrant and incumbent) to prevent intramodal price competition from driving prices to marginal cost and thereby precluding firm viability and (2) specific restrictions on supply (substitution between the markets served by the potential entrant and the incumbent) to prevent profitable hit-and-run entry. Examples of the first restriction come in the form of competition-reducing mergers, and examples of the second may be found in restrictions on competitive access (approvals of vertical foreclosures). In short, welfare-maximizing Ramsey prices are viewed as incompatible with enhanced contestability, and degradation of contestability to permit Ramsey prices in excess of marginal cost is viewed as welfare enhancing in the last three applications.

If movements toward perfect contestability via enhanced competition during the transition to deregulation lead to a "market meltdown" in the theory, what is the alternative? Chapter 5 discusses the alternative proposed by Meyer and Tye (1988), the "contractual equilibrium." It closes with a discussion of the achievements of contestability analysis in addressing the issues raised by a transition to deregulation.

NOTES

1. "The crucial feature of a contestable market is its vulnerability to hit-and-run entry." See Baumol (1982) and Baumol, Panzar, and Willig (1982).

2. See Baumol and Willig (1983a, 1983b) and Interstate Commerce Commission (1983). The ICC's views were based on the contestable market theories and were supported by 14 other prominent economists, including George Stigler, Almarin Phillips, Kenneth Arrow, Elizabeth E. Bailey, and Ann F. Friedlaender. See *Comments of Five Railroads* (1983) and AAR (1985).

3. The necessity to impose a lag in the pricing response of the incumbent in the postentry world was only implicit in the contestability model as initially specified in Baumol, Panzar, and Willig (1982, 5, 9, 11, and 361). Its crucial role appears to have been first observed by Dixit (1982), who noted that a lag is necessary to preclude the old incumbent from deterring entry by threatening to slash prices faster than the new incumbent can exit the market. The idea of permitting the entrant to achieve this lag via contracts with customers prior to entry apparently

came as an afterthought to the theory. For development of the concept of lagged price response by incumbents, see Bailey and Baumol (1984, 114–115); Brock (1983); Schwartz and Reynolds (1983); Baumol, Panzar, and Willig (1983, 492–493); Perry (1984); Bailey and Friedlaender (1982, 1040, 1041); and Stiglitz (1987).

4. See Baumol, Panzar, and Willig (1986, 341; 1982, 24–25) and Bailey and Friedlaender (1982).

5. See Baumol (1983a, 3–4):

> The entrant suffers no disadvantage in terms of production technique or perceived product quality relative to the incumbent . . . it is a requirement of contestability that there be *no cost discrimination against entrants* [emphasis added].

6. Entry barriers are defined by the theory of contestable markets to be "the additional costs that must be borne by an entrant just because he is an entrant rather than the incumbent" (Baumol and Willig 1983a).

7. Economies of scope arise if the "total costs to a carrier of supplying any services simultaneously [are] less than the sum of the costs of supplying them in isolation from one another" [footnote omitted]. See Willig (1983, 52) and Panzar and Willig (1977b). The presence of joint costs is one origin of economies of scope. See Panzar and Willig (1981). For a discussion of the application of the economy-of-scope concept to the rail industry, see Bailey and Friedlaender (1982).

8. The origins of the theory as applied to a monopolist operating under constant returns go back considerably. Samuelson (1947, 78–79) noted that with perfectly free entry a monopolist "would find its maximum advantage in behaving like a pure competitor." It is important to note, however, that Samuelson was addressing the case of the contestable monopolist operating in a range of constant costs, not decreasing costs, such as would usually characterize a contestable monopoly.

9. The situation where movements toward perfect contestability would eliminate any set of sustainable and viable prices is the most extreme case of the conflict between movements toward perfect contestability and achieving the Ramsey-efficient optimum. Even if the set of sustainable prices was not null, enlargements of the set via creation of impediments to contestability would be justified by the theory if a more static efficient Ramsey price set were made available (see Phillips 1980; Braeutigam 1979).

10. Note that this is an extension of the unsustainability problem first developed by Faulhaber (1975), which concerned the threat of "uneconomic bypass" that would raise total industry costs. The threat of entry can foreclose more Ramsey-efficient price sets for the sustainable monopolist as well.

11. "Transactions costs" are the legal and administrative costs of negotiating and policing sales agreements. See Alchian and Allen (1968, 469–472).

12. Economies of scope arise if the "total cost to a carrier of supplying any services simultaneously is less than the sum of the costs of supplying them in isolation from one another" [footnote omitted]. See Willig (1983, 52) and Panzar and Willig (1977b, 481–493). Joint costs are one origin of economies of scope. See Panzar and Willig (1977b, 268–272).

13. Baumol (1982) notes that the critical assumptions of the theory of contestable markets which applicants rely on are frictionless entry and exit and cost parity between incumbents and potential entrants:

> The entrant suffers no disadvantage in terms of production technique or perceived product quality relative to the incumbent. . . . It is a requirement of contestability that there be *no cost discrimination against entrants*. . . . Any firm can leave without impediment, and in the process of departure can recoup any cost incurred in the entry process. . . . *The crucial feature of a contestable market is its vulnerability to hit-and-run entry* [emphasis added].

14. See Willig (1979b, 346):

> This effect [''the smaller incremental cost . . . is enjoyed by the enterprise with the broader scope of production''] may cause *economies of scope entry barriers*. . . . The greater the degree of scope economies, the larger the cost disadvantage of a firm that offers fewer products. Moreover, *the wider the set over which economies of scope extend, the more product lines a potential entrant must plan in order to avoid these cost disadvantages* [emphasis added].

15. "Market dominance" is a term of art in rail rate regulation used to identify individual freight movements calling for regulatory review of rates. "Market dominance" is defined in the Interstate Commerce Act as "an absence of effective competition from other carriers or modes of transportation for the transportation to which a rate applies" (49 U.S.C. 10709[a]). Determinations of market dominance must be made by the ICC prior to assuming jurisdiction over the reasonableness of the rate according to the Staggers Rail Act, P.L. 96–448, 13 October 1980, 94 Stat. 1895.

16. Baumol and Willig (1983a, 1983b) and Baumol (1979). "The stand-alone cost test, in brief, requires that the consumer of a service be charged a price no higher than that at which it could be offered by a *specialized* competitive supplier" [emphasis added] (Baumol and Willig 1983a, 7). See also Baumol, Panzar, and Willig (1982, 352–353) and Faulhaber and Baumol (1988, 595–596).

17. Tye (1985b) shows that the hypothesized "group" SAC competitor will, in these circumstances, become a multiproduct firm with joint costs which must be allocated within the group before the SAC rate in question can be determined. But this is precisely the original joint-cost allocation problem which the SAC test proposes to solve on the entire railroad.

18. For a proposed alternative to SAC, see Meyer and Tye (1988).

19. Baumol, Panzar, and Willig (1982, 467) note that the first task in contestability analysis is to determine the cost-minimizing industry structure.

20. Note that the achievement of the purported welfare gain in vertical merger proceedings required the degradation of contestability because such efficiency gains were available only to the merged firm and thus became entry barriers to unaffiliated rivals in the postmerger world. Likewise, imposing a true "surrogate for contestability" would have foreclosed much of the price discrimination permitted by the more permissive SAC test. Both cases may thus be thought of as posing conflicts between achievement of static efficiency and contestability.

21. For example, see Meyer and Tye (1988).

22. Recent applications of contestability theory continue to reflect this ambivalence. Baumol (1984a, 217) noted "the important and legitimate point that if even one of the two pertinent markets is perfectly contestable, then vertical integration will not provide an opportunity for increased joint profits simply through rate

reduction." See, however, Baumol (1986a) for a later restatement of the claim of such pricing benefits in an actual merger proceeding in which the markets were alleged to be highly contestable. See also Baumol (1986b).

23. Note that the achievement of static efficiency gains in the application to vertical mergers also required a degradation of contestability.

2

Vertical Mergers into Contestable Markets

The closer one examines the concept of perfect competition the stronger are found to be the conditions for its validity. The horizon of perfect-competition prerequisites seems to be ever receding. Surely, the central position the concept of perfect competition has enjoyed since the 18th century is not about to falter. But the emphasis should be on its centrality as an organizing concept and certainly not as an innocuous descriptive category for the real world.

Mas-Collel (1982)

The theory of contestable markets has been invoked as support for regulatory decisions to immunize from further antitrust scrutiny a number of recent vertical (end-to-end) mergers in the transportation industries.[1] The theory is typically invoked in intermodal vertical mergers where a non-contestable railroad proposes to acquire a water carrier which is assumed to operate in a highly contestable market prior to the merger. The theory is also invoked in the case of intramodal rail mergers. The following propositions are said to follow from contestability theory even when one of the merging carriers possesses market power, so long as the other carrier operates in highly contestable markets prior to the proposed vertical merger:

1. The proposed merger will produce significant benefits of "pricing efficiencies"[2] and reduced "transactions costs,"[3] and such benefits can only be achieved via the proposed merger;
2. Pressures of contestability will force the merger benefits to be flowed through to the customer; and
3. Such merger benefits will not produce a "merger wave" among other similarly situated firms seeking to achieve the same benefits.

The theory of contestable markets[4] is also invoked to justify certain propositions about possible postmerger anticompetitive behavior. In recent proposed intermodal rail/water carrier vertical mergers,[5] the following propositions are offered:

4. The relevant markets where the water carrier operates prior to the merger are highly contestable, and postmerger contestability in those markets will not be degraded in any way by the proposed merger;
5. The merging railroad has no anticompetitive incentive to merge into highly contestable markets served by water carriers, because monopoly profits could have already been maximized via a "perfect price squeeze" established on the "bottleneck" railroad link prior to the merger;[6] concerns over postmerger anticompetitive vertical foreclosures of water carrier competition by the merging rail carrier are thus unfounded;
6. Since contestability cannot be degraded in water carrier markets by the proposed merger, concerns over postmerger predation and cross-subsidy by the merged carrier are unfounded; such practices would be impossible in a highly contestable market;
7. Because the newly integrated carrier cannot be motivated by any anticompetitive objective in its postmerger vertical relationships, there is no profit incentive for the newly merged firm (even when possessing monopoly power in the rail market) to deny access to the market by a more efficient, nonvertically integrated, competing water carrier;
8. The traffic will always move over the most efficient route; "voluntary negotiations" will produce the "parity principle,"[7] whereby the integrated carrier will always route the traffic via a more efficient, nonvertically integrated competing water carrier because its profits will be enhanced; and
9. Since the integrated merged carrier will always deal with a nonvertically integrated water carrier on a "neutral basis," any postmerger denials of competitive access or refusals to deal by the merged firm must be motivated by pursuit of efficiency gains.

Regulators should therefore promptly confer immunity from further antitrust scrutiny to the proposed merger according to the logic of these propositions.[8]

CONUNDRUMS IN THE MODEL

A possible conflict emerges between the theory of contestability as the answer to possible postmerger anticompetitive behavior and the nature of the *specific claims* of significant merger benefits advanced in these vertical merger proceedings. The assumption of a highly contestable market prior to the proposed vertical merger places extreme limits on the kinds of efficiency gains that are achievable by a vertical merger. The resulting conundrum may be seen intuitively as follows.[9] Demonstrating meaningful merger benefits *in the form of the particular efficiency gains claimed by applicants* requires the premerger existence of specific types of market imperfections that could be eliminated by the proposed merger, and only by the merger. But the ability to achieve the particular benefits claimed in these proceedings is not consistent with the assumption of a highly contestable market prior to the merger. To demonstrate the absence of any possible postmerger anticompetitive impacts, merger applicants sought to demonstrate that these same market imperfections were de minimis, both before and after the merger. Applications of contestability theory to these mergers have never figured out a way of satisfying both requirements simultaneously, and merger applicants switch from the assumptions of incontestable to highly contestable to support the nine propositions.

This intuitive discussion of the conundrum of demonstrating merger benefits in contestable markets can be clarified by examination of the economic model underlying these propositions. The model demonstrates that the logical difficulties arise not from an inherent contradiction in the theory of contestable markets, nor from poor empirical economics. Rather the difficulties originate from the same paradoxes that create ambivalence in the conventional theory of vertical foreclosure. There, one group of analysts explains restrictive practices merely as a search for efficiency gains, while another imputes anticompetitive intent. A third suggests that both may be at work. The extreme assumptions of contestability theory merely provide an idealized market paradigm where the reasons for the ambivalence in the economic theory of vertical foreclosure are seen more clearly.

This chapter provides a basic framework for analyzing the above nine claims in vertical mergers. In addition to questioning the reliance on contestability to give antitrust immunity to these proposed vertical mergers, the model points to paradoxes in more general theories supporting permissive approaches to vertical mergers and foreclosures of competition in vertical economic relationships which are pursued in Chapter 3.

Figure 2–1
Example of Typical Competitive Access Problem in Vertical Mergers

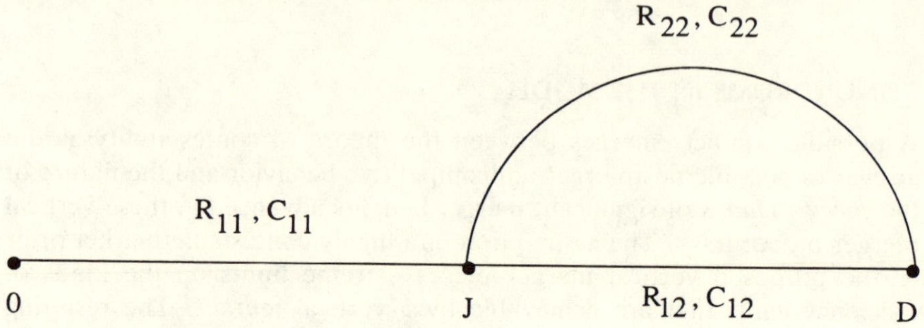

CLAIMS OF PRICING EFFICIENCIES

The easiest place to identify logical difficulties with the nine propositions as applied to recent vertical mergers is to examine the particular pricing efficiencies that were to be achieved as a result of a vertical merger. Prior to the merger, applicants state that individually established prices are inefficiently high for the respective portions of a combined end-to-end rail/water carrier movement because of what is generally called the "compounding of monopoly" problem.[10] After merging, it is claimed that a single integrated firm will charge a lower "joint rate" (the total rate over the through route from origin to final destination) than the sum of the "proportional rates" previously charged by the independent carriers on their respective segments of the "through route."

But if prices of at least one of the applicants in an end-to-end merger are already established optimally because of the efficiency properties of highly contestable markets,[11] there can be no meaningful premerger market imperfections in pricing to be eliminated as merger benefits in these circumstances. Because of the properties of highly contestable markets, prices in at least one of the markets are established at competitive levels by the threat of hit-and-run entry. Therefore, there is no anticompetitive pricing to be compounded when each carrier establishes its independent rate. Conversely, if these premerger market imperfections in pricing do exist, it is inconsistent to deny their postmerger existence when applicants claim the merged firm will continue to interline with unaffiliated carriers on a "neutral basis" after the merger because of the absence of market imperfections in a contestable market.[12]

Suppose, as shown in Figure 2–1, prior to the merger a railroad operates over a noncontestable route from an origin (point *O*) to a junction (point *J*) where it interchanges traffic with two water carriers operating from *J* to

D. The railroad's price for its respective portion of the movement is R_{11} and total cost is $C_{11} = S_{11} + C'_{11}V_{11}$, where V_{11} is the railroad's volume. It is assumed that substantial economies of scale and substantial sunk costs (S_{11}) require that prices necessary for "adequate revenues" (a term of art in railroading) for the rail portion substantially exceed the relevant incremental costs (C'_{11}). Entry by either of the water carriers into the rail market from *O* to *J* is assumed to be infeasible because of extreme barriers to entry.

Of the two water carriers shown in the figure from the junction to the destination, the first is assumed to be the merger applicant and the second is a "representative firm" from the "pool of potential entrants."[13] In the water carrier industry, it is assumed for the purpose of argument that there are many such identical firms serving other routes before and after the merger.[14] The two water carriers have production cost functions of

$$C_{12} = S_{12} + C'_{12}V_{12} \qquad (2\text{–}1)$$

and

$$C_{22} = S_{22} + C'_{22}V_{22}, \qquad (2\text{–}2)$$

where S_{12} and S_{22} are fixed and sunk costs,[15] and V_{12} and V_{22} are the respective volumes on the water routes. C'_{ij} is the per unit variable or marginal cost.

As discussed in Waterson (1982), the literature has produced conflicting conclusions regarding the consequences for economic welfare arising from pricing efficiencies made possible by vertical integration by an upstream monopolist. Researchers emphasizing the "compounding of monopoly" problem generally predict welfare gains resulting from the fact that a monopolist that integrates forward will eliminate the market imperfection arising from its own monopoly pricing and also produce likely reduction of prices and welfare gains in downstream markets. Other researchers have concluded that the results could go either way, depending on the relative magnitude of downstream pricing effects and the efficiency gains arising from eliminating inefficient downstream production methods which occur because of upstream monopoly in the premerger situation. The overall results are sensitive to the elasticity of final demand, elasticity of substitution between the monopolized input and other inputs to the downstream production, and competitive conditions in the downstream market (see Westfield 1981).

The complex welfare prescriptions of the economic literature when a monopolist integrates forward are greatly simplified in the example at hand. First, substitution possibilities between rail and water carrier services are assumed away. The principal issues posed by the claims of the merger applicants then become: (1) whether efficiency gains from reduced transactions costs (proposition 1) are possible; (2) whether the postmerger traffic is routed over the most static efficient water carrier (proposition 8); and (3) whether the price rises or falls for the sum of the two services after the merger (propositions 1 and 2). Second, as shown below, the possibility of pricing efficiency gains can be easily eliminated, leaving the only efficiency issues to be productivity gains and the choice of the most efficient postmerger water route. The static measure of welfare gain and loss offered by applicants[16] will therefore be accepted provisionally for the purpose of examining the above nine propositions.

Assume that both water carriers have identical cost functions prior to the merger and mutually contest one another's traffic. So with perfect contestability,[17] $S_{12} = S_{22} = 0$ and $C'_{12} = C'_{22}$.[18] Such contestability is frequently cited in vertical mergers, where carriers using identical technology to produce similar services over alternative routes could readily engage in hit-and-run entry if either carrier should choose a price such that $R_{12} > C'_{12}$ or $R_{22} > C'_{22}$, where R_{12} is the first water carrier's proportional rate for the water movement only and R_{22} is the second water carrier's proportional rate for the water movement only.[19] Let R be the "combination" rate, where $R = R_{11} + R_{12} = R_{11} + R_{22}$. For the purpose of argument, we also assume that prior to the merger, the traffic interchange entails transactions costs of $T_1 = T_2$ for doing business with the first and second water carriers respectively. The railroad's net revenues from doing business with the first (P_1) and second (P_2) water carrier prior to the proposed merger then becomes

$$P_1 = RV_{12} - C'_{11}V_{12} - R_{12}V_{12} - T_1, \text{ and} \qquad (2\text{–}3)$$

$$P_2 = RV_{22} - C'_{11}V_{22} - R_{22}V_{22} - T_2. \qquad (2\text{–}4)$$

Demonstrating the impossibility of pricing efficiency gains from a vertical merger given the assumption of perfect contestability and this pricing structure is relatively trivial, but will be done to illustrate the approach to the more difficult cases that follow. Assume that $T_1 = T_2 = 0$ and the railroad merges with the first water carrier. Suppose

$$R_{11}^{B} + R_{12}^{B} > R_{11}^{A} + R_{12}^{A}, \qquad (2\text{–}5)$$

where the superscripts indicate before-merger (B) and after-merger (A) proportional rates on the respective route segments.

A profit-enhancing cut in the final price on the through movement (the joint rate) by the merged carrier after the merger requires above profit-maximizing prices on both segments prior to the merger (if a profitable price reduction could be accomplished by reducing the rail price and the other market is contestable, that reduction must have been possible unilaterally even without the merger). But since a reduction in the price to a level below costs on the highly contestable segment after the merger would cause immediate exit from that market, we must have an after-merger reduction of price on the water route such that:

$$R_{12}{}^{B} > R_{12}{}^{A} \geq C'_{12}. \qquad (2\text{–}6)$$

The possibility of a profit-increasing reduction in price on the water route after the merger forces a contradiction: profitable entry could have occurred in the contestable market prior to the merger.[20] If postmerger reductions in the through rate are profitable and achievable only via vertical integration, the water carrier must not have been operating in a contestable market prior to the merger. Conversely, if prices equalled average costs in the contestable market prior to the merger such that profitable entry was foreclosed, profitable postmerger rate reductions on both the contestable route and on the through route are impossible.

CLAIMS OF TRANSACTIONS COST SAVINGS

In mergers involving purported highly contestable markets, applicants also rely on contestability analysis to support the claim that transactions cost reductions can be achieved in such a vertical merger between a firm operating in a contestable market and one operating in a noncontestable market without degrading contestability.[21] The types of transactions cost savings that are routinely cited by merger applicants are:

1. Fear of disclosing confidential marketing information to a competitor and a lack of trust; and
2. Designing long-term contracts between independent firms when the future is uncertain.

Likelihood of Transactions Cost Savings in Contestable Markets

Although less obvious than for the claims of pricing efficiencies, the efficiency properties of highly contestable markets also make unlikely the types of transactions costs that are claimed to be eliminated by the proposed vertical mergers. The simplest illustration of the logical difficulties arising from the claim of significant transactions cost savings in contestable markets is the willingness to share confidential marketing information, which merger applicants claim they, but not independent entities, will be motivated to do after the merger. To begin with, it is difficult to understand why an unwillingness to share confidential information would be a problem in a highly contestable market because the rail carrier could readily do business with another water carrier if the incumbent exploited a confidential relationship.[22] If the railroad were treating all water carriers "neutrally," including its own water carrier affiliate, all commercially relevant information must be as widely known as possible to enhance entry prospects of unaffiliated water carriers into the water route. (The possibility of hit-and-run entry requires that all competitively relevant information must be freely and equally available to both affiliates and entrants.)

In any event, transactions costs that are incurred to negotiate agreements to overcome a "lack of trust" would have little role to play in contestable markets. Significant transactions costs savings of the type cited are unlikely because buyers and sellers do not ordinarily need to spend significant sums negotiating and policing sales agreements to protect their interests from "opportunistic behavior" in highly contestable markets.[23] Indeed, buyers and sellers would incur transactions costs, while giving up the discipline of contestability during the term of the agreement for a commitment possibly subject to opportunistic behavior. Because there are no sunk costs idiosyncratic to the relationship, either firm could terminate the vertical agreement with no exit costs, and fear of opportunistic behavior is not a source of transactions costs.

Likewise, incurring transactions costs to negotiate long-term contracts to achieve an efficient allocation of risk between vertically related firms in the face of future uncertainty would appear to be inconsistent with the strong assumptions of contestability. The seller, exposed to the risk that future events might make the terms of the contract unattractive to the buyer, would insist that contestability be suspended for the long term of the contract in precisely the circumstances where entry would be attractive, that is, where the contract terms later proved unattractive to the buyer relative to the market prices offered by potential entrants.[24] If long-term contracts between vertically related firms are economically efficient, buyer and seller relationships would be governed by the terms of the contract, not by the threat of hit-and-run entry. Contestability would thereby be degraded (i.e., entrants could not contest incumbents' prices regardless of their efficiency advantages).[25]

Transactions cost savings simply do not seem promising via vertical integration into a highly contestable market. Rather, transactions costs are linked to enduring relationships which have little place in highly contestable markets.[26]

Consequences of Efficiency Gains from Vertical Mergers for Postmerger Contestability

It is, of course, possible that a vertical merger into a contestable market could produce economy of scope efficiency gains originating from other sources (say a new technology), rather than pricing and transactions costs savings. Such claimed efficiency gains might not expressly contradict the efficiency properties of contestable markets prior to the proposed merger.[27] Or pricing benefits and reduced transactions costs may be achieved only via the proposed merger (as claimed).[28] But if either such efficiency gains arise, they can be realized only where the merger alters the structure of the relevant markets by degrading their contestability (i.e., by creating efficiency advantages available to incumbents but not entrants). The reason is that applicants claim that the proposed merger confers competitive advantages to the merged entity that cannot be realized except by merger, but would not incite other firms to merge, that is, would not impose cost disadvantages on potential entrants whose competitiveness is necessary to keep the market contestable. In the theory of contestable markets, it is exactly such disadvantages to specialized potential entrants that create economy of scope barriers[29] to entry enjoyed by the incumbent.

Contrary to proposition 4, such postmerger efficiencies must degrade the postmerger contestability of the market if such economies are achievable only via merger as also claimed. To see this result, suppose that prior to the merger, both water carrier firms have equal operating costs and operate in contestable markets, and both incur equal transactions costs. To make the example interesting, assume that the merger between the noncontestable railroad and the water carrier reduces operating costs for the merged firm but leaves them unchanged for the railroad when interlining with the unmerged nonvertically integrated water carrier. We also assume that the merger itself incurs certain transactions costs that are sunk to the merger agreement, so that the role of the barge subsidiary is not contestable by former entrants into the water routes in question.

Propositions 1 through 9 now become inconsistent. The conflict arises from the mechanism by which the merged carrier chooses to move the traffic over the most efficient route after the merger in proposition 8. Assume initially that both sunk costs and transactions costs are zero. The model underlying the nine prospositions works under these assumptions via a "perfect price squeeze."[30] The merged carrier establishes the revenue division for the unaffiliated barge carrier equal to its own incremental costs when the vertically integrated firm is the more efficient carrier (thus foreclosing "uneconomic bypass") and equal to the connecting carrier's incremental costs "plus a peppercorn" when the competing water carrier is the more efficient:

$$R_{22} = C'_{22} + D_2, \text{ where } D_2 > 0 \text{ when } C'_{12} > C'_{22}; \qquad (2\text{–}7)$$

and

$$R_{22} = C'_{12}, \text{ when } C'_{22} \geq C'_{12};$$

where D_1 and D_2 are the division of the static operating efficiency gains between the integrated firm and the water carrier, respectively, from opening up a more efficient joint-line route:

$$C'_{12} - C'_{22} = D_1 + D_2 = D, \tag{2–8}$$

and

$$D_1 > 0 \text{ for all } D, D_2.$$

According to the theory, making the entrant hand over most of its static efficiency gains as the price of competitive access creates a profit incentive for the integrated firm to encourage entry of a more static efficient, specialized competitor.[31]

Assume again that the railroad merges with the first water carrier and that the railroad incurs transactions costs in interchanging traffic with the two water carriers (T_1 and T_2) prior to the merger. Define the unit welfare consequences resulting from reentry by the second water carrier to capture V_{12} to be

$$\frac{\Delta W}{V_{12}} = D_1 + D_2 + \frac{T_1}{V_{12}} - \frac{T_2}{V_{12}}, \tag{2–9}$$

where ΔW is the total welfare gain (savings in both operating efficiency and transactions costs) from successful entry to capture the incumbent firm's volume.[32] Let ΔW_1 and ΔW_2 equal the division of this welfare gain between the incumbent and new entrant, respectively:

$$\Delta W = \Delta W_1 + \Delta W_2,$$

where

$$R_{22} = C'_{22} + \frac{\Delta W_2}{V_{12}}.$$

Figure 2–2 shows the loci of the allocation of the welfare between the incumbent and new entrant resulting when the water carrier entrant is more, equally, and less efficient than the incumbent (depending on whether $\Delta W > 0$, $\Delta W = 0$, or $\Delta W < 0$, respectively). By definition, the southwest quadrant represents departures from contestability (cost disadvantages to the entrant).[33]

Prior to the merger, contestability reigned (no cost disadvantage to en-

Figure 2–2
Possible Allocation of Efficiency Gains in Routing Traffic via an Independent Water Carrier after Vertical Merger

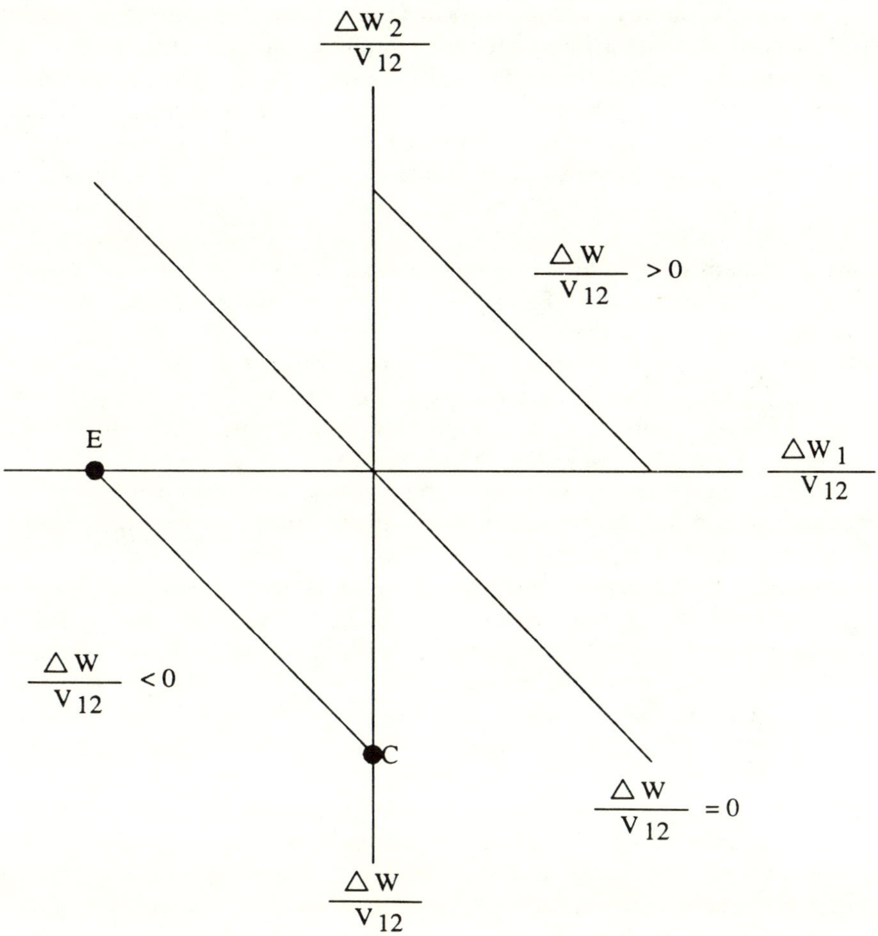

trants) and the only feasible competitive outcome was the origin. As a result of the merger, $T_1 = 0$ and the possible values of ΔW_1 and ΔW_2 are found in the southwest quadrant. Efficient routing of the traffic via proposition 8 above requires that $\Delta W_2/V_{12} = -T_2/V_{12}$, that is, the price of access be established such that the less efficient potential entrant be forced to absorb the entire burden of its new relative inefficiency. This is accomplished at point *C* in Figure 2–2. But the water route is no longer highly contestable by nonvertically integrated barge carriers at the postmerger division of revenues which is necessary for the merged carrier to route the traffic via the most efficient water carrier (namely, its own water carrier affiliate).

The new barrier to entry to the potential water carrier entrant is exactly equal to the economy of scope static efficiency gain to the merged carrier, that is, contestability is degraded by an amount equivalent to the new cost disadvantage to the entrant. The railroad earns additional profits on its newly acquired barge carrier while degrading by a like amount the ability of another water carrier to contest its routes.

Any attempt to make access available on a "neutral basis" (proposition 9) and to preserve the conditions necessary for contestability (proposition 6) will violate the parity principle (proposition 8) by making the integrated carrier establish R_{22} to absorb the potential entrant's relative inefficiency. This point is illustrated in Figure 2–2 at point *E*. At the revenue division that preserves contestability in the barge market by establishing a revenue division for the barge movement (R_{22}) equal to the average cost of potential entrants, there is no incentive for the railroad to hold open the joint-line route because it would be less profitable than its own single-line route (again by the amount of entrant's cost disadvantage).

Clearly, the pressures of contestability alone will not ensure that the merger benefits will be flowed through (proposition 2), given proposition 5 that monopoly profits can always be maximized and the fact that contestability will, in fact, be degraded. Of course, it may be true that, as with any monopolist, the rail carrier could make an even greater profit by reducing the rate on the through route (but not by the amount of the cost reduction occasioned by the merger).[34] But this will not eliminate the price squeeze on the unmerged water carrier necessary to ensure the traffic moves over the most static-efficient route.[35] Contestability is still degraded by the amount of efficiency gain, which the unmerged water carrier would have to bear fully if it were to attempt to contest the integrated carrier's volume.

These results may be illustrated by means of a simple hypothetical example. Suppose the rail rate is \$10 a ton and the two contestable barge firms each incur incremental operating costs of \$6 a ton and unit transactions costs of \$1 a ton. First, pricing gains are clearly unattainable as a result of merger. If the premerger through rate of \$17 could have been profitably cut by the merged firm, it would have been profitable for the railroad to cut its \$10 proportional rate prior to the merger (ignoring, for the moment, cost changes in order to focus on claimed pricing efficiency). The unaffiliated railroad would have realized the full benefit of any such rate cut because the pressure of contestability would force the barge line to charge the same \$7 regardless of the railroad's rate.

Next, we consider the possibility that the merged firm is able to eliminate the \$1 transactions cost. If the joint rate does not change, the merged carrier now earns gross revenues of \$11 on the rail portion of the single-line route, but the same $10 as before on the joint-line route. The rail carrier must either "refuse to deal" with the unmerged carrier by closing its route or reestablish the revenue division so that the joint route produces the same revenues to the merged firm as the single-line route. But the "parity principle" in this case produces only $6 in revenue for the unmerged carrier, insufficient to cover both operating expenses and transactions costs.

In the unlikely event that the merged carrier reduces the joint rate by the full amount of the efficiency gain, the results are the same. The merged carrier earns $10 on the single-line route, the same as before the merger. But the gross revenues on the rail portion of the joint-line route are reduced to $9. Since revenues have been reduced by $1, the only way to prevent an incentive to foreclose the joint route is to force the unaffiliated barge carrier to bear the $1 cut in rates entirely. The claimed efficiency gain can only be assured when it is accompanied either by a price squeeze of equal magnitude or by a vertical foreclosure (refusal to deal with unmerged rivals). Whether the benefits of reduced transactions costs are retained by the merged carrier or passed on all or in part, the answer is the same: achievement of the claimed efficiency gains requires degradation of contestability.

One suggested possible solution to the logical difficulties involved in advancing all nine propositions is that no market is perfectly contestable,[36] thus implying that they could be made consistent as the extreme conditions of contestability are relaxed. If this were true, it would be a strange result indeed, given the fact that perfect contestability is held up as the economic welfare optimum. If the welfare claims listed above became more true the more the facts departed from the assumptions, the results would certainly be bizarre.

In fact, the necessary degradation of contestability holds throughout the spectrum of contestability. This may be seen by reference to Figure 2–2. The departures from perfect contestability that are supposed to resolve the discrepancies are not specified, but may be thought of as a situation where barriers to entry preclude profitable entry of a more efficient carrier. In Figure 2–2, this is represented by a true welfare trade-off frontier in the northeast quadrant. Due to the assumed barriers to entry, the entrant perceives a trade-off lying in the southwest quadrant (including the origin).

The effect of a vertical merger in these circumstances is to create additional profits for the route of the integrated carrier without creating any offsetting additional incentives for profitable entry, that is, without eliminating the barriers to entry. Indeed, the net incentives for profitable entry are reduced, because the potential efficiency gains from entry are reduced while the barriers to entry are left unchanged. Contestability is still degraded by the amount of the efficiency gain (cost disadvantages to the entrant increase directly with the efficiency gain) while the departures from contestability that are claimed to solve the problem are unaffected by the vertical merger.

APPLICATIONS

The difficulties of supporting all nine propositions appear to be resolvable only by retaining a consistent subset of the above propositions. In actual merger proceedings, two candidates for deletion are either proposition 1 of meaningful merger benefits, or the combined claim of proposition 1 that the benefits are achievable only through merger and proposition 4 that contestability will be unaffected by such merger benefits.

Merger applicants, however, are reluctant to drop the claim of meaningful benefits achievable only via merger because the absence of such a claim would raise the question of what besides anticompetitive intent would be left to motivate the merger. Claims of substantial static efficiency gains from vertical mergers must, therefore, be carefully scrutinized because they may be of a type founded on the presence of market imperfections that are in turn denied when the possibility of anticompetitive consequences is rejected. Conversely, if anticompetitive possibilities are remote, requests to approve such mergers on the grounds that they promise substantial efficiency gains must be treated skeptically because the necessary premerger market imperfections may be de minimis. While approval of the requested antitrust immunity may not be harmful in such circumstances, the predicates for the claimed premerger inefficiencies must be carefully examined to ensure that they do not simultaneously contravene the assumptions made when concluding that anticompetitive consequences were de minimis.

Dropping proposition 4, which states that contestability will be unaffected by the merger, would appear initially to be more promising for merger applicants seeking to claim meaningful merger benefits. The analysis showed that contestability was necessarily degraded by the amount of the merger benefits, but the remaining assumptions may imply that customers are little affected. The reason was proposition 5, that the railroad was already charging a profit-maximizing price before the merger and would do so as an integrated firm afterwards. This means, of course, that contestability on the water route alone will not necessarily force the merged carrier to pass on merger benefits to customers. The postmerger degradation of contestability on the water route, however, becomes a matter of indifference to the shipper in the model because the premerger contestability on the water route did nothing to cure the lack of contestability on the rail route. According to the revised theory, consumer interests are preserved, not because contestability on the water route alone is preserved, but because contestability on the water route alone is irrelevant to consumer welfare (in the static framework assumed in these merger proceedings) as long as proposition 5 is true.

Assuming a proposed merger that promised demonstrable efficiencies that did not contravene the assumptions of a high degree of contestability prior to the merger, a possible response to the necessary degradation of contestability might be "so what?" According to the logic, the loss of contestability would not be troubling precisely because it is required to achieve the static efficiency gains.

The question can only be answered by a more thorough inquiry into the significance of the necessary degradation of contestability for the permissive economic model used to condone postmerger vertical foreclosures of unmerged rivals' access to the relevant markets ("refusals to deal"). Carriers offer proposition 9 to support their claim that they must cancel the competitive access of their rivals (engage in a vertical foreclosure) to prevent shippers from choosing inefficient competing routes, and these denials of competitive access are blessed by references to the permissive model.[37] But if propositions 5 and 8 are true, the price squeeze would have already made attempts to serve inefficient routes unprofitable to the nonvertically integrated barge carrier, precisely because the necessary degradation of contestability forces these firms to exit the market.[38]

Merger applicants, however, are extremely reluctant to concede that postmerger contestability is degraded by the efficiency gain, because the necessity to degrade contestability with refusals to deal (or other restrictive vertical practices) with inefficient unintegrated rivals is the central doctrine of the permissive model of vertical foreclosures (see Chapter 4). The degradation of contestability via the assumed price squeeze in the model automatically eliminates inefficient market structures and entry. But by the same token, it eliminates the defense that a postmerger vertical market foreclosure is necessary to prevent "uneconomic bypass" and other inefficient entry or vertical market practices. The necessary degradation of contestability as a result of the merger is thus no trivial matter to be lightly conceded by merger applicants.

The necessity to degrade contestability in order to achieve welfare gains from vertical foreclosures is further troubling because "the unifying analytical structure" of contestability "aspire[s] to provide no less than a unifying theory for the analysis of industrial organization" to replace the theory of perfect competition.[39] Any efforts in this example to achieve "competition on equal terms" or to restore contestability in the postmerger world necessarily results in a static welfare loss in this model. This conundrum involves competitive access issues that go beyond those that arise in merger proceedings and must be addressed in a wider framework of the entire theory of vertical economic relationships.[40]

The necessary degradation of contestability also suggests that analysis of the welfare gains from such vertical mergers should not be confined to the narrow static framework used by applicants to measure efficiency gains in these proceedings.[41] If the promised efficiency gains were thought to be achievable, they might incite a merger wave or a series of "defensive vertical mergers" that would change the contestability of the entire industry as well as the individual markets at issue in the proposed merger.[42] The resulting loss of competitive pressures might result in losses of dynamic efficiency over time that exceed the static efficiency gains. Of course, a reduction in transactions costs through vertical integration might accomplish greater rather than lesser dynamic efficiencies. Regardless of the predicted long-run outcome, the necessary degradation of contestability points to the limitations of the static approach to welfare gains usually employed in these proceedings.

EXTENSIONS

The crucial role of transactions costs in evaluating efficiency gains and anticompetitive consequences of restrictive practices in vertical economic relationships was recognized long before contestability theory was offered as a "unifying analytical structure" for resolving antitrust concerns.[43] The potential anticompetitive consequences previously identified by the transactions cost approach, however, were generally limited to strategic purposes for restrictive vertical market practices and enhanced oligopolistic interaction.[44] In the example of recent vertical merger proposals, achievement of the promised efficiency gains of reduced transactions costs necessarily degrades contestability. The complete reliance by contestability theory on potential entry as the answer to possible anticompetitive concerns therefore raises serious questions regarding broad claims for a permissive approach to such practices based on the theory.

The framework developed in this chapter provides a basis for further explorations into paradoxes of vertical economic theory generally. The claims of efficiency gains which are used to justify vertical mergers and vertical foreclosures must not depend on the existence of market imperfections that are simultaneously denied when examining the possibility of anticompetitive consequences. Satisfying both requirements in practice turns out to be more difficult than is generally assumed in permissive attitudes toward these practices. The difficulties encountered in crafting the required premerger market imperfections in a sufficiently narrow manner in vertical mergers suggest the possibility of similar dilemmas in vertical foreclosure theory generally.

For example, the received permissive theory explains vertical foreclosures by the desire for efficiency gains because upstream monopoly profits are already assumed to be achieved through a downstream price squeeze. But the necessary loss of contestability from the price squeeze in the example of vertical mergers automatically forces the exit of inefficient unintegrated competitors and eliminates the "efficiency defense" for postmerger vertical foreclosures. The necessary degradation of contestability from vertical mergers in these circumstances thus has more than theoretical significance. These difficulties will be further illustrated by extending the above methodology in the next chapter to examine permissive approaches to vertical foreclosures in competitive access disputes in the rail industry.

NOTES

1. For case studies of applications of the theory to vertical mergers, see Baumol (1983a); Baumol (1984b); Baumol (1986a); Huneke, Lane, and McNamara (1985); and Shepherd (1988).

2. For the origin of the elimination of the compounding of the monopoly problem as a rationale for vertical merger, see Spengler (1950). More generally, see Warren-Boulton (1978) and Blair and Kaserman (1983).

3. "Transactions costs" are the administrative and legal costs of negotiating and policing a sales agreement. See Alchian and Allen (1968). Transactions costs savings are recognized as a source of efficiency gain from vertical mergers and restrictive vertical practices that are often disapproved of by the antitrust laws. See Williamson (1974, 1979).

4. The conclusions regarding competitive impacts of vertical mergers may be more accurately thought of as an application of the Chicago School permissive approach toward vertical mergers and vertical foreclosures. See Posner (1978–1979) and Bork (1969, 1978).

5. Similar conclusions were also offered for end-to-end intramodal rail mergers. The analysis that follows on rail/water carrier mergers because of the agreement that water carrier markets were more contestable than rail markets. The analysis is extended to the case of imperfect contestability in Chapter 3.

6. See CSX (1986);

> Where one entity in a combination has market power, it already has the opportunity and incentive to exercise that market power by charging the optimal profit-maximizing price. No effort by the newly consolidated firm to raise prices could increase profits; for the company with market power would already have exercised that power by establishing the optimal rate for its separate service.

For hypothetical examples of the perfect price squeeze where a bottleneck rail carrier competes with a connecting rail carrier, see Tye (1987c), and Chapter 3 below.

7. See Baumol (1983b), Tye (1986b), and Marshall and Cook (1986).

8. In these practical applications, approval by the ICC foreclosed challenges to the merger in the courts on traditional antitrust grounds.

9. See also Tye (1985a, 1984c).

10. See Warren-Boulton (1978) and Baumol (1983b) for illustrations of the principles.

11. Contestability is deemed to be desirable because such markets exhibit four desirable attitudes:

> The four key performance attributes of perfectly contestable markets are: (1) in the long run no excess profits can be earned in such a market; (2) no inefficient

> firm can survive in such a market; (3) no cross subsidies can persist; and (4) predatory pricing must be unprofitable.

See Baumol (1986a, 4–6, 41).

12. Contestability theory is cited by merger applicants when arguing that:

> 1. Bilateral ''voluntary negotiations'' between the merged carriers and unaffiliated water carriers will *always* produce the best of all possible worlds in the post-merger competitive environment and these relationships can be safely left to the workings of the marketplace; therefore, there need be no regulatory concern for postmerger vertical foreclosures of competition; and
>
> 2. Substantial benefits can be realized by an end-to-end merger of the applicants because the merger would eliminate the inefficient pricing and operating practices that *necessarily* have arisen from individual negotiations between the merger applicants themselves.

Baumol and Willig (1985b) state that "all that is required" is to permit the two independent vertically related firms to engage in voluntary negotiations "to co-ordinate pricing on terms freely agreed upon."

13. See Bailey and Baumol (1984).

14. See Boger (1985). Baumol, Panzar, and Willig (1983) show that any arbitrary subsets of exchanges in a competitive market are contestable. Thus we focus on the two firms assumed to be serving the route prior to the merger. The merger affects the contestability of all unmerged potential entrants in the "pool" similar to the second unintegrated barge carrier actively competing prior to the merger on the water route in question in the example.

15. Contestability analysis allows for a circumstance where costs are fixed but not sunk, the case of the "contestable monopoly." See Baumol and Willig (1981). Since these terms will be equated to zero below, the distinction is not relevant to the issues raised in Chapter 2. In Chapter 3, this assumption is relaxed. The significance of positive transactions costs is also considered.

16. "Static efficiency" in this context thus comes down to cost comparisons based on "variable costs" of the traffic on alternative routes and is the measure of economic welfare used to defend the permissive approach to vertical foreclosure in these merger proceedings. The measure, of course, ignores dynamic (long-term) welfare gains and losses and does not consider downstream welfare gains and losses resulting from the effect of the merger on prices (volume is assumed constant). The "incremental costs" which are relevant to static efficiency concerns over the routing of particular traffic have commonly been equated to the (per unit) variable costs on the route in disputes over competitive access. Of course, actual routing decisions should be based on total logistics cost and service differences. These could be added to the analysis to increase the generality of the results without affecting the basic conclusions. More generally, making the movement of traffic over the most static efficient route the only determinant of policy produces rather peculiar recommendations for competitive access in a transition to deregulation in the rail industry. (See Chapter 3.) If the rail carriers have the same incremental costs, the connecting rail carrier is forced out of business by the denial of access, but the loss of competition is judged to be of little concern. In contestability analysis actual competition among incumbents has no welfare significance in the presence of hit-

and-run entry. Likewise, if one rail carrier has a cost disadvantage, that route is forced to exit the market and all the traffic goes to the other route. Making static efficiency in routing traffic the only goal in establishing competitive access policy results in the implausible conclusion that competition among incumbents is redundant when the conditions for a competitive equilibrium of equally efficient firms are satisfied and possibly harmful when it is not. Such a limited goal would hardly be the recipe for a successful transition to deregulation in an industry with substantial sunk costs or where a merger wave threatened to degrade substantially the contestability of the industry.

17. In the spirit of the claims that water routes are highly contestable and that the theory of contestable markets is highly applicable to these mergers, we begin with the limiting case of perfect contestability claimed by merger applicants. These claims by applicants were in fact resisted by opposing water carriers, but are accepted here for the purpose of examining the internal consistency of the nine propositions. This assumption is relaxed in Chapter 3.

18. This assumption satisfies the requirement in contestable markets that "there be no cost discrimination against entrants." See Baumol (1982).

19. Carriers must agree on a "through route" through the junction (i.e., a joint service agreement) for the traffic to physically move. The rail carrier must agree on a "joint rate" from *O* to *D* or publish a "proportional" rate from *O* to *J* as well. Note that R_{11} and R_{12} are undefined in the absence of a joint route and revenue division agreement between the carriers, for example, a situation of vertical foreclosure or refusal to deal.

20. Note that such claims of pricing efficiencies in these circumstances are also at variance with proposition 5 that the carrier in the noncontestable market need not merge with the water carrier to exploit all the profit there is to be had even without the merger.

21. See Baumol (1983a; 1983b; 1984a, 217).

22. It might be argued conversely that there is no deterrence to a breach of confidentiality by the water carrier, since cost-free exit would prevent the railroad from punishing a water carrier who violated confidentiality.

23. When vertically related firms sink costs into specialized investments that are idiosyncratic to the relationship, the resulting quasi-rents are said to be "appropriable" by "opportunistic behavior" (i.e., a "hold up") designed to change the income shares specified by the terms of the relationship. Contracts are usually signed in competitive markets to eliminate such incentives. For discussion of the role of specialized sunk costs in creating short-term monopoly power to practice opportunistic behavior between vertically related firms, see Klein, Crawford, and Alchian (1978). More generally, see Fitzroy and Mueller (1984) and Williamson (1985).

24. Incurring transactions costs to negotiate contracts that will protect the interests of sellers is offered as the answer to imperfections in contestability that would prevent an incumbent from retaliating before the contestant could exit the market. See Baumol (1986a, 40, 49–50). This answer, however, unreasonably assumes that the incumbent makes no strategic use of such contracts to prevent entry. See Aghion and Bolton (1987, 388–401) and Stiglitz (1987).

25. See Baumol, Panzar, and Willig (1982, 291):

> Future contracts that assure the entrant that his sunk outlays will not be wasted can reduce that problem, so that at the time the contracts are being negotiated they can decrease the size of the entry barrier which the sunk cost would otherwise entail [footnote omitted]. But in doing so they substitute a new and more formidable entry barrier during the life of the contract, by precluding any further potential entrants from the business that the contract has tied up. The greater the length of time for which the contract holds, the lower will be the risk of the initial entrant when he sinks his cost, so the lower will be the magnitude of entry barriers at the time of contract negotiation. But the longer the life of the contract, the longer the later entry barriers will endure.

26. Note that the presence of positive transactions costs in equations (2–3) and (2–4) would convert the water carrier market into a natural monopoly where the most efficient market structure would require that all traffic be carried by one water carrier. Such costs would be an example of costs that are "fixed" over volume and "sunk" over time (the duration of the contract). Such costs could be positive in the theory of contestable markets only if they are fixed but not sunk (not idiosyncratic to the specific transaction). Either such fixed costs are idiosyncratic to the transaction and thus sunk, or the seller will insist that they be made so by contract. The difficulties of specifying positive transactions costs that do not violate the assumptions of perfect contestability illustrate a more general difficulty in practice of specifying costs that are fixed but not sunk. See Chapter 4.

27. For example, the merger could possibly improve efficiency by preventing the barge subsidiary from violating confidentialities on the rail side of the business. This possible efficiency gain would not necessarily contradict the assumption of contestable water routes.

28. The key assumption in the above example that prevented the possibility of pricing efficiency gains was the fact that all water carriers established separate proportional rates prior to the merger. If the railroad established a joint rate for the through route taking the proportional water rate as given by contestability, efficiency gains in pricing would also be impossible. The only case where efficiency gains in pricing might be possible is where the water carrier established the joint rate and the rail rate exceeded marginal cost. The possibility of such pricing efficiencies would arise from the fact that the internal transfer price for the rail movement for the integrated firm would be rail marginal cost rather than the monopoly price. But these inefficiencies could be eliminated by the rail carrier, who could successfully undercut the water carrier's joint rate by offering one of its own without vertically integrating. For analysis of this special case, see Quirmbach (1982, 6), who nevertheless concludes that "when the upstream monopoly is protected—and when in addition forward integration is partial and upstream marginal costs constant in the relevant range—the external [rail proportional rate in this example] and final goods prices [joint rate in this example] always rise."

29. See Willig (1979b, 346):

> This effect ["the smaller incremental cost . . . is enjoyed by the enterprise with the broader scope of production"] may cause *economies of scope entry barriers. . . .* The greater the degree of scope economies, the larger the cost disadvantage of a firm that offers fewer products. Moreover, *the wider the set over which economies*

of scope extend, the more product lines a potential entrant must plan in order to avoid these cost disadvantages [emphasis added].

30. See McFarland (1987), Tye (1987c), and discussion below for examples. A price squeeze is not simply an incidental or unintended consequence of the application of the voluntary negotiations theory to the competitive access problem. Such negotiations work to eliminate routing inefficiency according to the theory only if the price squeeze on the unaffiliated connecting carrier is "perfect" or sufficiently so. See Ordover, Sykes, and Willig (1985).

31. With no sunk costs and perfect contestability on the competitive link, there is no incentive for entry by an equally efficient connecting carrier under the pricing rule. Under the assumptions of contestability theory, the threat of entry alone is sufficient to achieve the optimum welfare properties of the model. No additional beneficial role is assigned to actual competition rather than potential competition.

32. Note that in contestability theory, a more efficient entrant can capture all the incumbent's volume instantaneously with a slight change in price.

33. Note "it is a requirement of contestability that there be no cost discrimination against entrants." Entry barriers are costs incurred by entrants but not by incumbents. See Baumol (1983).

34. Whether this will be true or not has generated a significant literature that shows that contestability on one route is not sufficient for price to fall. See Warren-Boulton (1978) and Salinger (1988). Westfield (1981) sums up the results of the new research by noting that with regard to the effect of vertical integration on downstream prices, "the results are not easily summarized." In an unpublished paper, Quirmbach (1982) shows that vertical integration between a vertical upstream contestable monopolist into a downstream competitive industry that charges a final price to the consumer will produce an unambiguous welfare gain. The gain results because the integrated firm is able to price the input to its own subsidiary at marginal cost, thereby eliminating the price distortion of average cost pricing of the input prior to the merger, and pressures of contestability force the complete pass-through of the welfare gain. When the downstream market is incontestable, Quirmbach's results show that proposition 2 cannot be unambiguously predicted.

35. To show that the necessary price squeeze is invariant to the amount of efficiency gain passed on in the form of a price decrease on the postmerger joint rate, assume in the extreme that it is all passed through (see proposition 2). The merged carrier will, according to the parity principle (proposition 8), leave the operating income on the rail movement intact, thus forcing the revenue division for the barge movement to bear the full impact of the price decrease. Since unaffiliated barge carriers' costs are unaffected, contestability is thereby degraded by the amount of the gain passed through to shippers.

36. Baumol (1984a, 217).

37. See Baumol and Willig (1985a, 1985b, 1985c) and Willig (1984b).

38. The "perfect price squeeze" automatically forecloses "uneconomic bypass" as shown above. The need for vertical foreclosure to achieve efficiency gains thus becomes highly questionable, because the perfect price squeeze necessary for monopoly profits also forces the exit of inefficient nonvertically integrated firms.

39. See Baumol, Panzar, and Willig (1982, 320–321) and Baumol (1984).

40. Vertical mergers illustrate a common paradox in many applications of con-

testability theory, whereby departures from contestability are frequently labeled as welfare enhancing. For more on this phenomenon, see Chapters 3 and 4. See also Stiglitz (1981).

41. For a discussion of some of these issues, see Tye (1987).
42. See Ordover and Willig (1983, 571).
43. See, for example, Williamson (1974, 1439) and Phillips (1975, 573).
44. Williamson (1979, 953–954, 960).

3

Sunk Costs, Transactions Costs, and Vertical Foreclosures in the Rail Industry

In today's orthodoxy, "economic theory" is seen as beyond refutation by mere evidence and experience.

Culbertson (1986)

The theory of contestable markets has recently been cited in support of permissive attitudes by regulators and the courts toward denials of competitive access (vertical foreclosures) in the rail industry. Yet these same theories have elsewhere been contrarily cited in support of regulatory action to promote competitive access. Puzzling discrepancies have also arisen between the behavior predicted by the permissive model of vertical foreclosures and fact in the rail industry.[1] A close examination of these recent applications reveals both insights into unresolved problems with the theory of contestable markets and, more generally, paradoxes in the typically permissive views of the economic literature toward vertical foreclosures of competition and vertical integration (Blair and Kaserman 1983).

This chapter attempts to clarify these baffling differences in policy recommendations and the puzzling discrepancy between theories and fact in the rail industry. The results suggest that these puzzles can best be solved by applying concepts central to the theories of the Chicago School[2] and contestability theory: the presence of transactions[3] and information costs and substantial sunk costs.[4]

First, the discrepancies that have arisen in practice in the rail industry are explored in some detail so that the reader can get a flavor of the paradoxes which these theories have produced. Then the chapter formalizes the permissive theory when the implicit assumptions of zero transactions/information and sunk costs are valid. This formalization of the permissive model is somewhat tedious, but absolutely necessary to understand the puzzling discrepancies. The analysis demonstrates that with zero transactions costs, zero information costs (perfect information), and no sunk costs (perfect contestability), the permissive model of vertical foreclosure in the rail industry is partly justified. However, violation of these assumptions in the rail industry creates incentives for opportunistic behavior to appropriate competitors' revenues necessary to amortize sunk costs, predation, cross-subsidy, denials of competitive access to more static efficient competitors, and incentives to merge for (quasi-) "rent seeking" objectives rather than enhancement of efficiency.

Figure 3–1 illustrates these results in more detail for a variety of cases, depending on the particular combination of assumptions. Most notably for case 1, the formalization demonstrates that the permissive model is not logically consistent even when its assumptions are satisfied. Some but not all of the propositions advanced by the permissive theory necessarily follow from the necessary assumptions. When the formal model is then extended to the more realistic assumptions (at least in the rail industry) of positive sunk costs (case 2), the static efficiency properties of the permissive model are retained, but a successful transition to deregulation is threatened. The conclusions for cases 3 and 4 may be thought of as extensions of the "Coase theorem" on transactions costs[5] and Oliver Williamson's application of the theories of bounded rationality.[6] The chapter then proposes a rule for opening up competitive access in the rail industry in order to address the problems created by the violation of the assumptions of the permissive model and considers some of the objections to this rule. In addition to explaining why behavior in the rail industry does not conform to the permissive model, examination of the consequences of violations of the assumptions of the permissive model points to ways of thinking more clearly about vertical mergers and foreclosures generally.

SOME BAFFLING DISCREPANCIES IN THE APPLICATION OF THE PERMISSIVE MODEL TO THE RAIL INDUSTRY

Recent applications of the theory of contestable markets to provide a model[7] to regulators in the rail industry represent the most elaborate application of the theory to vertical economic relationships and illustrate most pointedly the issues. Of particular importance is the issue of competitive access, that is, cancellations or unilateral denials of intercarrier operating agreements. These cancellations or denials have the effect of "foreclosing"

Figure 3–1
Structure of Alternative Assumptions Regarding Permissive Model of Vertical Foreclosures in Rail Industry

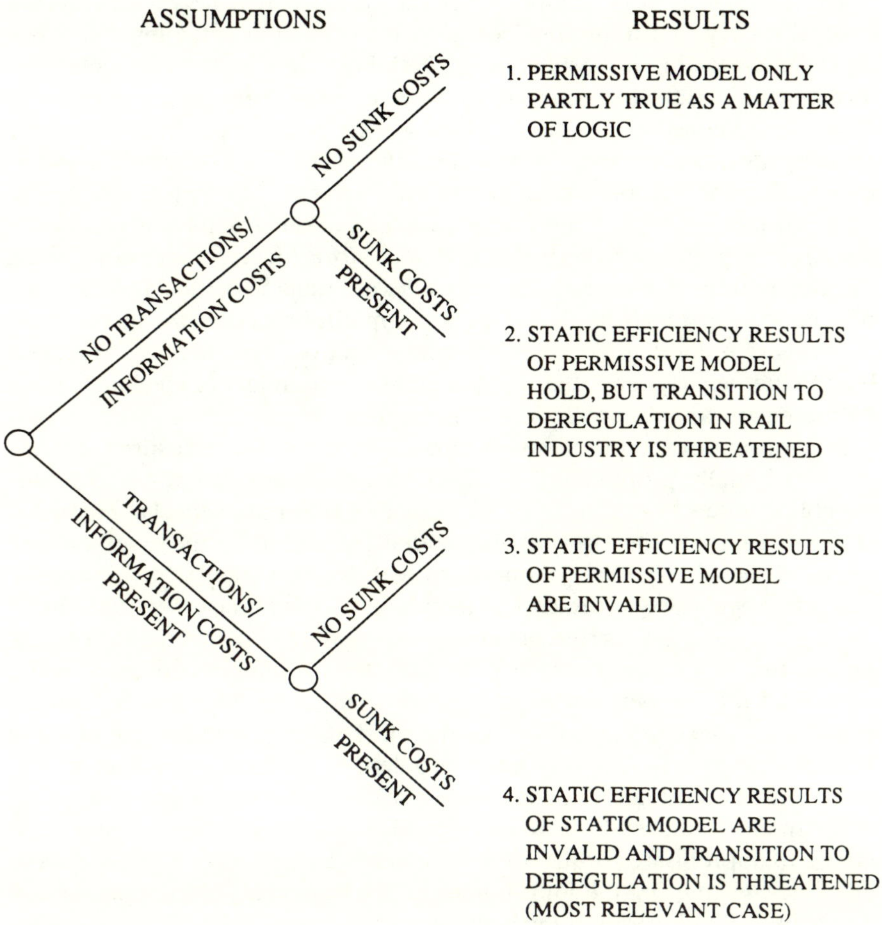

the ability of one of two vertically related ("end to end") carriers to compete in a relevant market for rail transportation.[8]

The competitive access problem takes on special significance in the rail industry because lack of competition on a "bottleneck" or "essential facility" in the integrated service network could be used to foreclose competition which must be maintained on other portions of the rail system during a successful transition to deregulation.[9] The rail industry is characterized by customers with shipping facilities that rarely interconnect with more than one carrier, substantial volumes of joint-line traffic, limited possibilities for entry, and the presence of substantial sunk costs. Competitive access to "bottleneck" facilities on equal terms is thus generally believed to be critical to preserving and promoting intramodal competition in a deregulated rail industry.[10]

The Chicago School theory of vertical foreclosures, however, offers a general theory that minimizes concerns over possible anticompetitive behavior in vertical relationships by (1) defining "anticompetitive" chiefly in terms of reductions in economic welfare resulting from price increases in downstream consumer markets, (2) assuming zero transactions costs and perfect information, and (3) assuming the ability to extract all possible monopoly profits at one stage in a vertical relationship with a sufficiently high price. Since (4) any inefficient vertical market structure or practice is a source of profit and there is no obstacle to achieving that profit given the assumptions, the necessary conclusions are that (5) vertical foreclosures of competition (such as denial of a competitor's access to an essential facility) are redundant as a tool of monopolization, and rarely, if ever, can lead to inefficiency, and that (6) such denials can in fact be explained only by the desire to enhance economic efficiency.

In a variant of the permissive approach to vertical foreclosures of competition initially propounded by the Chicago School, the theory of contestable markets has been cited in approval of actions to cancel competitive access (hereafter, the "permissive model"). Combining the essential elements of the Chicago School approach with the new theory of contestable markets, regulators were advised to rely upon "voluntary negotiations"[11] among the involved carriers, even in a deregulated environment. The rationale that was initially offered was that static economic efficiency is the only relevant competitive access concern and such negotiations can be relied upon to route the traffic over the most efficient carrier. Use of static inefficient routes is allegedly not a problem in a regime of voluntary negotiations, because a bottleneck carrier with market power can, according to the theory, make even more money by using a threat to deny competitive access to appropriate for itself the benefits of a competitor's greater static efficiency when using the joint-line route. In any event, market power was not believed to be important because the threat of hit-and-run entry by motor and water carriers ensured that the relevant markets would remain highly contestable. Regulatory actions to open up competitive access in the rail industry (for example, via trackage rights after mergers to cure anticompetitive consequences) in an effort to make rail markets as contestable as possible were viewed as the "worst possible remedy that a malevolent mind could devise."[12]

Contrarily, contestability analysis also has been cited to express reservations about a permissive approach to the denials of competitive access. The theory of contestable markets has previously been offered to support regulatory intervention to ensure that limitations on competition at one stage of vertical relationships in markets undergoing a transition to deregulation not be allowed to foreclose competition at a prior or subsequent stage. The basic idea was that regulators in an industry seeking a transition to deregulation should implement policies that approximate the results of a contestable market. Regulators, "rather than relying exclusively on traditional rate and entry regulation," should pursue "government intervention to ensure equal access to the sunk facility," so that all firms seeking such competitive access should get it, and so that "the access price be reasonable."[13] Bailey (1981, 179, 182) applied these concepts to urge consideration of open competitive access via trackage rights in the rail industry.

These dramatic differences in policy recommendations arising from the same theory pose disturbing questions in developing a consistent policy toward competitive access. The tendency of rail carriers (1) to engage in vertical foreclosures by cancelling joint routes and other intercarrier operating agreements regardless of static efficiency considerations and (2) to pursue mergers designed to enhance opportunities for vertical foreclosures that cannot be explained entirely by efficiency motives will be shown below to be another puzzle for the permissive theory on vertical foreclosures.

Indeed, one of the principal developers of the Chicago School theory, Judge Richard A. Posner, remanded Conrail's cancellations of route connections with other rail carriers to the Interstate Commerce Commission (ICC) for further review, citing Conrail's "grossly aggregative" approach to the pursuit of efficient vertical market structures and its reliance on a "meat ax approach" to cancelling intercarrier cooperative agreements with competitors.[14] Judge Posner recognized that Conrail had cancelled virtually every opportunity of its competitors to participate in the movement of traffic regardless of relative efficiency.[15] This indiscriminate behavior could not be explained by the Chicago School doctrine, which would call for a route-by-route assessment of relative efficiency, which the ICC was instructed to require Conrail to implement.

New research[16] also showed that the widespread permissive attitude by economists toward vertical foreclosures is not always justified. The set of assumptions required to support the conclusion that such behavior in unregulated industries could only be explained by efficiency gains was more restrictive than originally believed. The conventional theory assumed the existence of a "perfect price squeeze"[17] even without the alleged foreclosure, and there are four circumstances where this might not be true:

> (a) there is an alternative, albeit inferior, source of supply for the monopolized product; (b) profit-maximizing implicit price discrimination requires a low price for the monopolized product and a high price for complementary products; (c) inflexible rules govern prices or the division of revenues between the dominant firm and the producers of complementary

Figure 3–2
Example of Typical Competitive Access Problem in Vertical Foreclosures

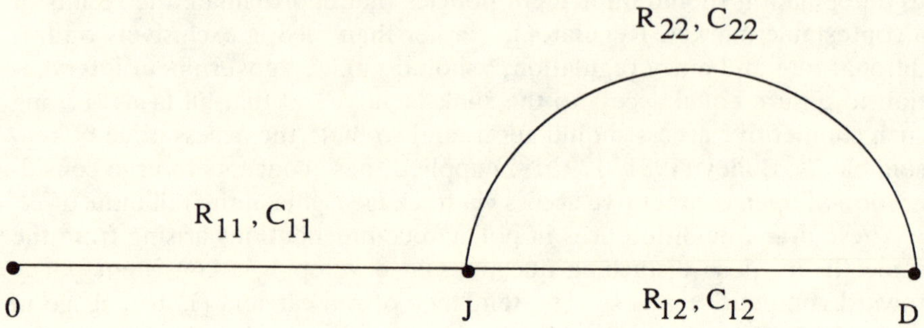

components; or (d) the dominant firm is subject to comprehensive rate of return regulation.[18]

The reasons for this ambiguity toward vertical foreclosures in the economic literature may be clarified by a formalizing of the necessary assumptions of the permissive model. The model demonstrates that the logical difficulties and conflicting policy recommendations arise not from an inherent contradiction in the theory of contestable markets nor from a failure to apply the model consistently. Rather, the difficulties originate from the same paradoxes that create ambivalence in the conventional theory of vertical foreclosure, where one theory explains restrictive vertical practices as a search for efficiency gains, while another usually imputes anticompetitive intent. The extreme assumptions of contestability theory merely provide an idealized market paradigm where the conflicts are seen with greater clarity.

WELFARE RESULTS OF THE PERMISSIVE MODEL IN THE ABSENCE OF SUNK COSTS, TRANSACTIONS COSTS, OR INFORMATION COSTS

Figure 3–2 illustrates a hypothetical example of a railroad competitive access problem in the typical format of the dispute (only two carriers are ordinarily involved). The first railroad, RR_1, sometimes also referred to as the "bottleneck carrier" or the "single-line carrier," operates from an origin (node *O*) to a destination (node *D*) via a junction (node *J*).[19] The second railroad, RR_2, sometimes referred to as the "connecting carrier" or the "joint-line carrier," operates only from node *J* to node *D*, and seeks "competitive access" to through traffic from *O* to *D* via a traffic interchange and joint rate agreement with RR_1.[20] Entry by the second carrier on the

Table 3–1
Carrier Long-Run Profit Functions as Determined by Routing of Traffic

	Single Line	Joint Line
P_1	$R_{11}V_{11} + R_{12}V_{12} - C_{11} - C_{12}$	$R_{11}V_{11} - C_{11} - T_1$
P_2	0	$R_{22}V_{22} - C_{22} - T_2$

route from O to J is assumed to be infeasible because of barriers to entry. Let R_{ij} be the per unit revenue (commonly referred to as a "revenue division") of the ith railroad over the jth route, such that for any particular movement:

$$R = R_{11} + R_{12} = R_{11} + R_{22}, \tag{3–1}$$

where R is the total unit revenue for the through movement in equilibrium. These revenue divisions are endogenous to the model.[21] Carriers also have operating cost functions over each link, C_{ij}, referring to the ith railroad over the jth link. These cost functions allow for costs of S_{ij} per unit of time which are both sunk (cannot be recouped by shutting down entirely) and fixed[22] (do not change in the short run with traffic volume)[23] over the competitive link:

$$C_{12} = S_{12} + C'_{12} V_{12}, \text{ and} \tag{3–2}$$

$$C_{22} = S_{22} + C'_{22} V_{22}, \tag{3–3}$$

where V_{12} and V_{22} are the volumes moving via the single-line and joint-line routes, respectively. C'_{ij} is the per unit variable or marginal cost[24] and is the measure of static economic efficiency used in the permissive model to measure welfare gains and losses arising from vertical foreclosure in the rail industry.[25] Table 3–1 shows the long-run profit function (P_i) of the ith carrier as it is affected by the routing of traffic and the existence of information and transactions costs by the ith carrier, T_i. Information costs are incurred by the carriers in learning their respective variable costs on the competitive and monopoly routes. Transactions costs are incurred in the process of negotiating R_{22}, the connecting carrier's per unit revenue division for joint-line traffic.

The permissive conclusions about vertical foreclosures arising from the model are based on the assumption that transactions, information, and sunk costs may be safely ignored, that is,

$$S_{12} = S_{22} = T_1 = T_2 = 0. \tag{3–4}$$

The logic of the permissive model is as follows. If the joint-line route is more efficient, that is, when

$$C_{12}/V_{12} > C_{22}/V_{22}, \tag{3–5}$$

then it will pay the single-line carrier to use the joint-line route whenever

$$C_{12}/V_{12} > R_{22} > C_{22}/V_{22} \tag{3–6}$$

because it is more profitable for the bottleneck carrier:

$$R_{11}V_{11} - C_{11} > R_{11}V_{11} + R_{12}V_{12} - C_{11} - C_{12}. \tag{3–7}$$

Under these assumptions, when the joint-line route is more static efficient than the single-line route, there will always exist a revenue division that at least covers the connecting carrier's average cost while saving the single-line carrier money and thus increasing net revenues.[26] On this basis, it is claimed that any regulatory intervention must be based on an assumed irrationality by the single-line carrier, since it will always be in the interest of the bottleneck carrier to grant access to a more efficient entrant so that it may appropriate some or most of its efficiency gain. Conversely, it is claimed that given such profit maximization, regulatory interference could easily result in forcing open a less efficient route which would otherwise be closed by the bottleneck carrier.

The proof is straightforward. We have assumed that the carriers operate in contestable markets, that is, $S_1 = S_2 = 0$. The necessary R_{22} may be established by the bottleneck carrier using the following rule. Let

$$R_{22} = C_{22}/V_{22} + D_2, \text{ where } D_2 > 0 \text{ when } C_{12}/V_{12} > C_{22}/V_{22}; \tag{3–8}$$

and

$$R_{22} = C_{12}/V_{12}, \text{ when } C_{22}/V_{22} \geq C_{12}/V_{12} \tag{3–9}$$

where D_1 and D_2 are the division of the static efficiency gains between RR_1 and RR_2 respectively from opening up a more efficient joint-line route:

$$C'_{12} - C'_{22} = D_1 + D_2 = D \tag{3–10}$$

and

$$D_1 > 0 \text{ for all } D, D_2.$$

The effect of the "voluntary negotiations" pricing rule in these circumstances is for the carrier controlling competitive access to give the connecting carrier a profit incentive to provide the service when it is the more static efficient and to force the connecting carrier's revenue division below its average cost when it is less static efficient. With no sunk costs and perfect contestability on the competitive link, there is no incentive for entry by an equally efficient connecting carrier under the rule.[27]

Since the bottleneck carrier sets D_2 at the minimum level necessary to induce entry, this amount may be thought of as a "peppercorn." Given the assumptions of contestability, only a trivially small potential profit would be necessary to create incentives for "hit-and-run" entry.[28]

Possible loci of D_1 and D_2 as a function of C'_{12} and C'_{22} are given in Figure 3–3.[29] When the carrier desiring competitive access has incremental costs equal to that of the single-line carrier, then $D = 0$, and there is no opportunity for static efficiency gains via use of the joint-line route. The efficiency frontier passes through the origin in this case. Since both carriers are assumed to have zero exit costs and are equally efficient, the only feasible point is the origin. When the connecting carrier's incremental costs are less than that of the bottleneck carrier, the trade-off possibilities lie in the northeast quadrant (between points E and G). The line through the southwest quadrant represents situations where entry by the connecting carrier would raise total industry variable costs, the so-called "inefficient bypass" or "unsustainability" problem (Panzar and Willig 1977). Such static inefficiencies are not a possibility under the strong assumptions made here. From these pricing equations, the following propositions of the permissive model are said to follow:

1. A perfect prize squeeze:[30] any trivially small $D_2 > 0$ will be sufficient to induce efficient entry in a contestable market; so the single-line carrier appropriates most of the connecting carrier's efficiency gains as the price of competitive access.
2. There is no profit incentive for the bottleneck carrier to foreclose entry of a more efficient competitor, that is, a sufficiently small $D_2 > 0$ exists such that $D_1 > 0$ whenever $C'_{12} - C'_{22} > 0$.
3. The "parity principle"[31] is satisfied: the single-line carrier's net revenue on a more efficient joint-line movement will always exceed its net revenue on the single-line movement; equal or lower net revenue would discourage the carrier from agreeing voluntarily to the joint-line movement when it is less efficient.
4. Denials of competitive access (refusals to deal) cannot be anticompetitive because monopoly profits could have already been maximized via the prices established by the bottleneck railroad for the total service and competitive access to the connecting carrier; the single-line carrier's

Figure 3–3
Efficiency Frontiers for Joint-Line Route for Alternative Possible Relative Static Efficiencies

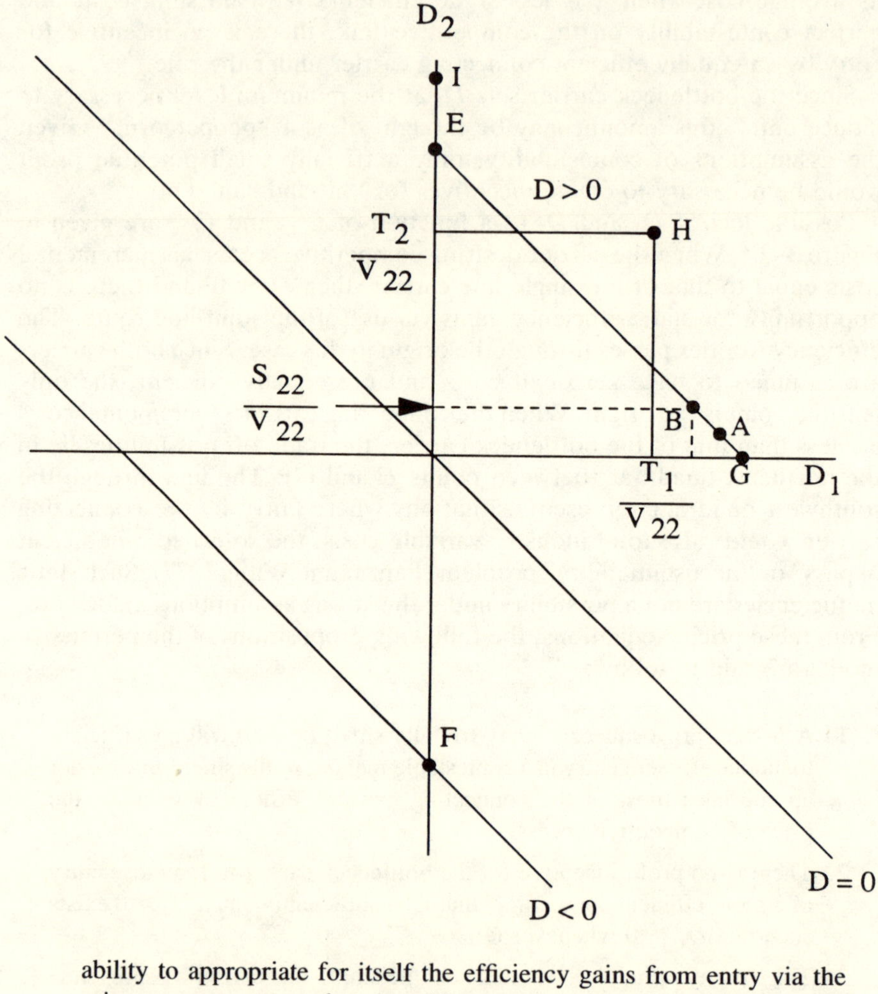

ability to appropriate for itself the efficiency gains from entry via the price squeeze means that the ultimate consumer has nothing to gain from any regulation designed to preserve competitive access for the connecting carrier.[32]

5. Traffic is always routed over the most static efficient route, which follows from propositions 2 and 3 and their converse: $D_2 < 0$ whenever $C'_{22} > C'_{12}$.
6. The bottleneck carrier will deal with the connecting carrier on a "neutral basis": there is no incentive for cross-subsidy or predation because the

equally or more efficient connecting carrier will always recover its total costs and the carrier controlling access has a profit incentive to encourage efficient entry.

7. Any regulatory constraint on these pricing rules and profit motives[33] could lead to inefficiency.
8. Since there is no incentive for vertical integration or denials of competitive access to enhance monopoly profits, the only logical explanation for such behavior must be the pursuit of static efficiency gains.

These eight propositions have become the implicit intellectual reference point for the Interstate Commerce Commission's permissive policy toward vertical foreclosures in the rail industry. Below we investigate whether the assumptions are valid and the logical implications of violating the assumptions. But an internal logical difficulty already emerges in the propositions. The last two propositions do not follow from the assumptions of the basic model. Indeed, they must be replaced with two new propositions which fundamentally alter the analysis:

7N. The above six propositions hold reciprocally in a world of zero transactions and information costs and do not depend on which carrier is granted the right to apply the perfect price squeeze.[34]

8N. If there is no incentive to deny competitive access to enhance monopoly profits, neither is there a necessity to apply a vertical foreclosure to enhance static efficiency. (If $C'_{12} - C'_{22} < 0$, then $D_2 < 0$ for all $D_1 > 0$.) The ability to apply a perfect price squeeze makes a vertical foreclosure redundant as a means of enhancing monopoly profit, but, by the same token, it also makes a vertical foreclosure redundant as a means of achieving efficiency gains.

Proposition 7N not only points to a logical difficulty in the permissive approach; it also explains why the model fails to predict actual behavior accurately in the rail industry. In a world of zero transactions and information costs, regulatory constraints would affect the division of static efficiency gains between the two carriers, but not affect the static efficiency properties of the model. As long as efficiency gains are achievable via voluntary negotiations, any regulation that holds open the joint-line route becomes a "bargaining chip" that will be traded away at zero transactions costs in pursuit of efficiency gains. If such costless negotiations fail to produce efficient outcomes, there may be something wrong with the initial assumptions of zero transactions and information costs which support the permissive model.

Nor do the assumptions of the model support proposition 8's claim that outright cancellations of competitive access, defended on the grounds of their necessity to enhance efficiency, are necessary in the rail industry.[35] According to proposition 4, such denials would be redundant as tools of monopolization. But, according to proposition 5, *a vertical foreclosure would be also redundant in achieving efficiency*. But as discussed above, Judge Posner noted that Conrail relied on outright refusals to deal (cancellations of competitive access) rather than a perfect price squeeze to eliminate routes it claimed to be inefficient. And it applied the cancellations to all routes across the board on the basis of carrier identity, not just to specific traffic and routes where a disaggregate analysis indicated that it had a relative static efficiency advantage (using what Judge Posner described as a "meat ax" approach). This behavior was simply not consistent with the permissive model. Nor does the model explain why shippers vigorously oppose these cancellations of competitive access (McFarland 1987), directly contrary to proposition 4.

Conversely, if, according to proposition 8, vertical foreclosures are needed to enhance static efficiency, as claimed by carriers when closing competitors' routes, a perfect price squeeze must have not been available to establish a revenue division that would already have made such inefficient routes unprofitable to the connecting carrier, as claimed by propositions 1 and 5. This in turn implies, contrary to proposition 8, that such foreclosures might not be redundant as tools of monopolization and might even lead to inefficiency, as denied by proposition 2. As it turns out, such is the case when the assumptions necessary for the perfect price squeeze are relaxed.

Figure 3–4 illustrates three alternative relative efficiency relationships possible under the permissive model using the hypothetical examples in Baumol and Willig (1985b). Example 1 illustrates a case where the efficiency frontier passes through the northwest quadrant in Figure 3–3. Examples 2 and 3 illustrate the southwest quadrant and origin frontiers, respectively, in Figure 3–3.

Table 3–2 illustrates the operation of the price squeeze in the voluntary negotiations model for each of the cases in Figure 3–4. Note that in example 1 the bottleneck carrier earns almost $2 more by appropriating the connecting carrier's efficiency advantage rather than simply foreclosing access. But note also that the same efficient result would have been produced if the bottleneck carrier were to receive delta and most of the $12 were to go to the connecting carrier because regulators had forced the bottleneck carrier to give preferential routing to the joint-line route. As long as voluntary negotiations will produce an optimal routing, the reciprocity of proposition 7N holds.

Even more importantly, note that example 2 in Table 3–2 illustrates that the price squeeze makes a vertical foreclosure redundant as stated in proposition 8N. The less efficient connecting carrier need not be denied market access when it has a $1 static efficiency disadvantage. The price squeeze

Figure 3–4
Hypothetical Examples of Routing Efficiencies

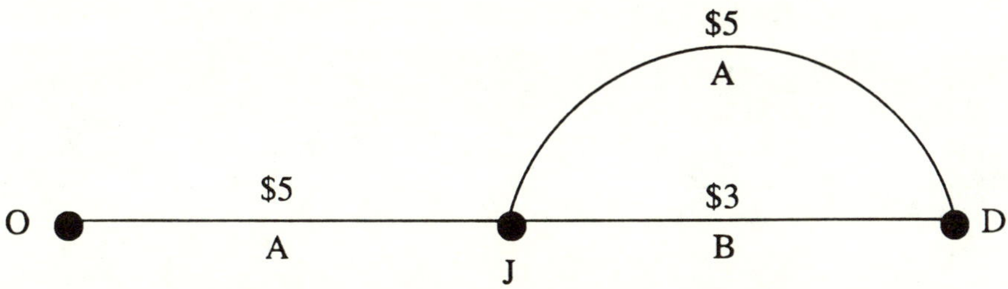

Example 1: Joint-Line Route Has Lowest Incremental Cost

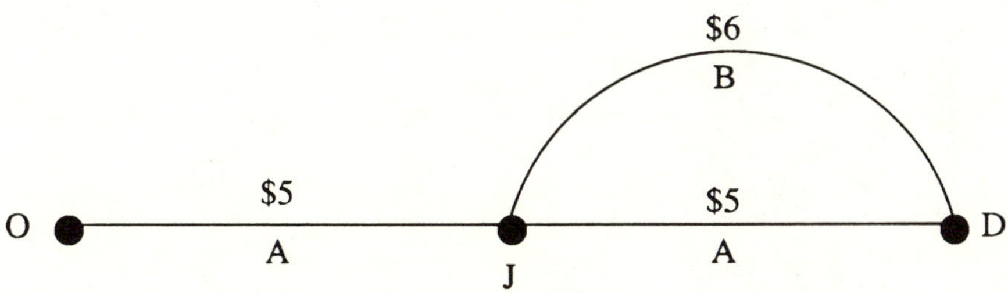

Example 2: Single-Line Route Has Lowest Incremental Cost

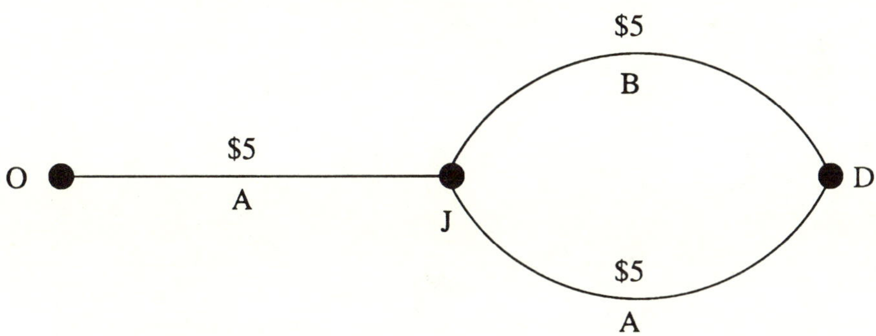

Example 3: Both Routes Have Same Incremental Cost

Note: Revenues for traffic over all routes are assumed to be $20.

necessarily makes the route unprofitable. Conversely, if the less efficient connecting carrier finds it profitable to compete, and must be foreclosed to achieve efficiency gains, the model's assumptions of a perfect price squeeze must be invalid.

Table 3–2
Net Revenues and Revenue/Variable Costs of Alternative Routes in Hypothetical Examples: Voluntary Negotiations Proposal with Price Squeeze

	Single-Line Route		Joint-Line Route	
Carrier	Net Revenues	Revenue/ Variable Cost	Net Revenues	Revenue/ Variable Cost
		Example 1		
A	\$10	2.0	\$12 -Δ	3.4
B	0	--	Δ	1.0
Total	\$10	2.0	\$12	2.5
		Example 2		
A	\$10	2.0	\$10	3.0
B	0	--	-1	0.83
Total	\$10	2.0	\$ 9	2.0
		Example 3		
A	\$10	2.0	\$10	3.0
B	0	--	0	1.0
Total	\$10	2.0	\$10	2.0

Source: See Figure 3-4.

To untangle these difficulties with the permissive model, we first relax the assumption of zero sunk costs. As shown in case 1 in Figure 3–1, the presence of sunk costs does not modify the static efficiency properties of the permissive model, but it does create another problem: The single-line carrier's price squeeze will make it impossible for the connecting carrier to recover its total cost. Conversely, any attempt by the single-line carrier to establish a price of access that permits the survival of the connecting carrier will eliminate the static efficiency properties of the permissive model and create an incentive for the single-line carrier to engage in a vertical foreclosure. The inability of a more efficient connecting carrier with sunk costs to recover total costs and survive is a serious fault of the permissive model if regulators are seeking to guide an industry with high entry barriers to deregulation.

THE ROLE OF SUNK COSTS IN THE PERMISSIVE MODEL

Assume now that $S_{12} > 0$ and $S_{22} > 0$, so that the relevant markets are no longer highly contestable.[36] Indeed, to give more realism to the example, assume that both carriers previously sunk their costs with the understanding that R_{22} would be established by prior rules agreed to by the carriers and reviewed by regulators.[37] Now let ratemaking be abruptly deregulated and regulators state that they will rely on voluntary negotiations and make no effort to enforce the rules on revenue divisions for joint routes previously in effect when the carriers sank their costs.

As long as we assume transactions costs are zero, the static efficiency properties of the previous results (propositions 1–6, 7N, 8N) will not be affected. Static efficient competitors are not foreclosed from recovering their variable costs, the parity principle is satisfied, traffic moves over the most static efficient route, regulatory intervention is not needed to ensure static efficiency, the results are reciprocal, and the right to foreclose competition is redundant as a means of achieving static efficiency.

However, these static efficiency results do not depend on incentives for entry as before, but rather on the existence of sunk costs as a barrier to exit (the inability of either carrier to exit the market without forfeiting its sunk costs). The new assumptions will still achieve a perfect price squeeze, but the static efficiency inducing revenue division to the connecting carrier need only ensure the recovery of the connecting carrier's variable costs. Unlike the previous situation of contestability, there is no guarantee that a more static efficient connecting carrier will recover its total cost. Such recovery of total costs is not necessary according to the theory precisely because the definition of sunk costs means that they need not be recovered to avoid immediate exit of a more static efficient connecting carrier.

The bottleneck carrier will be highly motivated to engage in "opportunistic behavior" (Klein, Crawford, and Alchian 1978) (i.e., a "hold up") to exploit the fact that the connecting carrier has sunk costs but no longer has a division agreement to protect its interests. It will now set the revenue division to a more static efficient connecting carrier such that:

$$C'_{12} > R_{22} = C'_{22} + D_2 \qquad (3\text{–}11)$$

where D_2 again is a trivially small sum.

Indeed, the bottleneck carrier *must* engage in such opportunistic behavior in a world of voluntary negotiations if it is to satisfy both the parity principle and the incentive to choose the most static efficient route.[38] The inherent conflict between RR_1's incentives for static efficiency and RR_2's recovery of its sunk costs under voluntary negotiations is shown in Figure 3–3. Assume initially that static efficiency gains from using the joint-line route are large relative to RR_2's unit sunk costs. All divisions of the benefits of the efficiency of the joint-line move that are necessary to keep a more efficient connecting carrier "revenue adequate" (a term of art in railroading where the carrier recovers both variable and sunk costs) fall between B and E where $D_2 > S_{22}/V_{22}$. But since the connecting carrier has sunk its costs, the bottleneck carrier will apply a perfect price squeeze and choose a point such as A where $0 < D_2 < S_{22}/V_{22}$. The connecting carrier has no alternative but to accept this offer because it cannot recover its sunk costs via refusal of the offer and exit from the market, and a trivially small D_2 is better than nothing.[39]

The result is an appropriation of most of the more static efficient carrier's sunk costs as well as its efficiency advantages, made possible only by a unilateral cancellation of the previous agreement for revenue divisions. The more static efficient connecting carrier would never have entered the market and sunk its costs in the absence of regulation without a contract with specified revenue divisions that would prevent this opportunistic behavior. At a minimum, this appropriation would seem an unfair shift in the rules relied upon by the more efficient connecting carrier when sinking the costs necessary for entry into the industry.

Furthermore, such a result creates a dilemma in the theory of voluntary negotiations as the answer to vertical foreclosure in the rail industry with its large sunk costs: if pricing above incremental costs is necessary for revenue adequacy (Baumol 1983b), it is likely that the bottleneck railroad cannot (1) be squeezing the connecting carrier's revenue division down close to its incremental costs so as to make itself the recipient of almost all net revenues under the joint-line route (so that it will have an incentive to use the more static efficient route) while at the same time it is (2) allowing the connecting carrier a sufficient division of revenues so that it is able to price sufficiently above its incremental costs to achieve revenue adequacy as well.

The price squeeze required by the permissive model would result in a cross-subsidy from a competitive market to a monopoly market and certainly looks predatory to the victim, even if it does not result in short-run losses to the single-line carrier.[40] The revenue division is certainly "predatory" in the sense that a more static efficient connecting carrier cannot recover its sunk costs which it needs to survive in the long run.

The likelihood of a cross-subsidy may be seen by examining Figure 3–3. Suppose the prior scheme of revenue divisions under regulation had ensured that the more efficient connecting carrier received a division that allowed it to amortize its sunk costs (say, point *B*). After the price squeeze, the service is provided by RR_2, but it is being forced to provide a cross-subsidy to the bottleneck carrier when the division is at *A*.[41]

It might be argued that the bottleneck carrier's appropriation of the connecting carrier's sunk costs should be of little interest because they are irrelevant to the future. Precisely because recovery of these costs is not necessary for a more efficient connecting carrier's willingness to provide the service in the short run, perhaps competitive access policy should be indifferent to the plight of the connecting carrier. If the connecting carrier goes bankrupt, the bottleneck carrier can acquire the estate which is made to be worth only peppercorns (plus scrap value) because of the price squeeze it has applied. New carriers might still be willing to enter the market because they would not invest without new traffic interchange agreements that would protect them from the plight of the previous defunct incumbent.

But the price squeeze necessary to create an incentive for the bottleneck carrier to pursue static efficiency gains has serious consequences for a successful transition to deregulation in an industry such as railroads with large sunk costs. The competition among incumbents that was the rationale for deregulation could be extinguished by relying on voluntary negotiations, thereby threatening the goal of relying on competition rather than regulation in a transition to deregulation. In an industry such as railroads with high barriers to entry, reestablishing the eliminated competition might be quite difficult if not impossible. Reregulation might become necessary. The notion that static efficiency gains are the only issues that are relevant to competitive access cannot be accepted when sunk costs and barriers to entry are significant in an industry such as railroads, which is in a transition to deregulation.[42]

One possible answer[43] that has been given to cure this defect of the permissive model is to argue that the single-line carrier would voluntarily establish $R_{22} = C_{22}/V_{22}$ (i.e., choose point *B* in Figure 3–3 rather than point *A* in Figure 3–3) in order to assure the long-run viability of the more efficient connecting carrier. The foresighted bottleneck carrier is assumed to be motivated to keep a more efficient carrier in business so that it can continue to capture its efficiency gains as the price of competitive access. But this proposal ignores the fact that the "perfect price squeeze" is more profitable for the bottleneck carrier in the long run and the short run. The single-line carrier can appropriate both the connecting carrier's static efficiency gains and its sunk costs (less the peppercorn) as the price of access at no cost to itself. There is no need for the bottleneck carrier to grant a division at *B* when it can unilaterally impose the more profitable point *A* in Figure 3–3. Should the inability of the connecting carrier to recover sunk costs in the short run result in its prospective failure, the bottleneck carrier need only offer to buy it out at "bargain basement prices" (the capitalized value of D_2) as discussed above.

Furthermore, this proposed solution contradicts the initial rationale of why the perfect price squeeze is necessary to achieve static efficiency gains. Should the bottleneck carrier attempt to keep a more static efficient connecting carrier revenue adequate so that $D_2 = S_{22}/V_{22}$, it may well have a disincentive voluntarily to route traffic over the more static efficient joint-line route in the short run.[44] The reason is that the profit of the bottleneck carrier on the less static efficient single-line route may be more than the bottleneck carrier's net revenue division on the joint-line route when that division is set low enough to allow recovery of the connecting carrier's sunk costs. Even when the single-line route is less static efficient, the bottleneck carrier will be motivated to use it as long as $R_{22} > C'_{12}$. The bottleneck carrier will be motivated voluntarily to use a more efficient joint-line route only when RR_1's extraction of RR_2's efficiency gains on the joint route fortuitously exceeds the loss of net revenues which it must give up to ensure the recovery of RR_2's sunk costs:

$$D_1 > S_{22}/V_{22}. \tag{3–12}$$

The latter will be untrue whenever the connecting carrier's sunk costs are large relative to the static efficiency gains it can offer to the bottleneck carrier as the price of competitive access. Such an outcome is illustrated by point *I* in Figure 3–3, which represents the net revenues necessary for the connecting carrier to recover sunk costs. Because sunk costs are large in the rail industry, a voluntary decision by the bottleneck carrier to allow the connecting carrier to recover total costs would as a general rule be infeasible as well as contrary to the bottleneck carrier's interests (except in the most extreme cases of efficiency differences). The proposal would ironically be infeasible precisely in the situation where competition is regarded as having the most important role to play in the long run and in contestability theory, that is, where carriers have equal costs.

Perhaps it is contemplated that a two-part compensation scheme could be designed whereby the bottleneck carrier would pay a fixed sum to allow the more efficient firm to recover its sunk costs in the longer run while maintaining an incentive in the short run to route the traffic over a competitor's more static efficient routes. But, once again, making a lump-sum payment of the competitor's sunk costs is not as profitable as the course of opportunistic behavior described above.

These points may be illustrated by reference to the hypothetical example in Figure 3–4 and Table 3–2. Suppose the more efficient connecting carrier and the single-line carrier in example 1 have unit fixed costs of \$3 a ton on the potentially competitive route when each carries the entire volume. The more efficient connecting carrier thus has a revenue requirement of \$6 a ton to remain viable in the long run. At this revenue division, however, it is more profitable for the single-line carrier to cancel the connecting carrier's competitive access and simply use its own less efficient single-line route. Indeed, it must engage in the price squeeze shown in Table 3–2 if it is to have an incentive to employ the most efficient route. Only in the fortuitous situation where the connecting carrier is so efficient that its total cost is less than the single-line carrier's incremental cost will it be possible to satisfy the objectives of the parity principle, efficient routing, and revenue adequacy of the most efficient carrier.

THE ROLE OF TRANSACTIONS COSTS AND INFORMATION COSTS IN CREATING INCENTIVES FOR VERTICAL FORECLOSURES

The preceding section demonstrated that the presence of sunk costs will not blunt the price squeeze necessary for the static efficiency results of the permissive model, but the squeeze will likely prevent the connecting carrier from recovering its sunk costs in the short run and highly likely from surviving in the long run. As shown in Figure 3–1, case 4,[45] we next demonstrate that lack of knowledge about the magnitude of the static efficiency gain (information costs)[46] and costs associated with negotiating the price of access (transactions costs) can make the appropriation of a competitor's static efficiency gains difficult or impossible.[47]

To see how, assume now that transactions and information costs are positive ($T_1 > 0$, $T_2 > 0$). Traffic will be routed over the more static efficient joint-line route, even in the short run, only when the static efficiency gains are sufficient to offset the transactions and information costs incurred when the bottleneck carrier appropriates them for itself.

Assume the joint-line route is more efficient. Then the single-line route provides less net revenues for the bottleneck carrier, that is,

$$R_{11}V_{11} + R_{12}V_{12} - C'_{11}V_{11} - C'_{12}V_{12} < R_{11}V_{11} - C'_{11}V_{11} - T_1, \quad (3\text{–}13)$$

only if static efficiency gains outweigh transactions and information costs required for the bottleneck carrier to appropriate them for itself:

$$T_1/V_{22} < D_1 \text{ and } T_2/V_{22} < D_2. \quad (3\text{–}14)$$

The combined assumptions of positive transactions and information costs thus can affect the validity of the conclusion that voluntary negotiations will always assure static economic efficiency as measured by variable costs. The failure of voluntary negotiations to assure the efficiency results will happen whenever $D_1 < T_1/V_{22}$ or $D_2 < T_2/V_{22}$, or both, for all feasible D_1, D_2, T_1, T_2. Point H in Figure 3–3 illustrates such an outcome where transactions and information costs incurred in applying a price squeeze block static efficient entry. The bottleneck carrier's necessity to extract a more efficient carrier's efficiency gains thus imposes transactions/information costs that can act as barriers to efficient entry. In the more realistic situation where the assumptions of the permissive model of zero transactions and information costs are violated, revised propositions apply:

1′. There may be no "perfect price squeeze" ensuring that the static efficiency gains from using a more static efficient connecting route exceed combined transactions and information costs when the bottleneck carrier extracts them for its own benefit.

2′. The single-line carrier will foreclose access of a more static efficient carrier whenever $D_1 < T_1/V_{22}$ for all feasible D_1, D_2.

3′. The parity principle is not necessarily satisfied, because providing competitive access to a more static efficient competitor may require reduction of the bottleneck carrier's net revenues.

4′. Prices to shippers can possibly be reduced in this scenario by regulatory-imposed access rules (see below).

5′. Traffic does not necessarily move over the most static efficient route. (Sufficiently large transactions costs of a price squeeze mean that $D_1 < T_1/V_{22}$ even though $C'_{12} > C'_{22}$.)

6′. If access is granted, incentives for cross-subsidy and predation in the presence of sunk costs will be exacerbated.

7′. Regulatory constraints can enhance competition and improve efficiency to the extent they encourage recovery of total costs by a more efficient connecting carrier and eliminate the transactions and information costs incurred by the bottleneck carrier in appropriating the connecting carrier's efficiency gains.

7N′. The results are reciprocal if the same transactions costs obstacles to static efficiency would apply to any rule that gave the joint-line route a prior claim to the traffic.

8N′. Whenever the transactions and information costs of employing a price squeeze are relatively high, firms will have (quasi-) "rent seeking" incentives for vertical integration in order to appropriate downstream competitor's sunk costs and efficiency gains without incurring the transactions and information costs of a price squeeze. If large transactions costs necessitate outright refusals to deal with inefficient competitors, they can also be sufficiently large to create incentives to deny competitive access to more static efficient competitors.

These principles may be illustrated again by reference to Figure 3–4. Suppose the bottleneck carrier has no direct knowledge to determine which of the thousands of shipments it could interline falls within the three categories identified in Figure 3–4. Suppose further that it must hire a consultant to explain the permissive model to its own pricing officers and those of its competitors, to conduct an exhaustive cost study of its own costs and that of its competitors, and to conduct the necessary negotiations to appropriate its competitors' efficiency gains. Suppose further that the carrier determines that it expects that the consultant's fee will amount to $2.01 for every ton found in example 1 in Figure 3–4. The bottleneck carrier in this example will find it more profitable simply to cancel competitive access of all competing carriers regardless of relative efficiency considerations rather than to apply the price squeeze. Sufficiently large transactions costs in effect convert example 1 to a situation equivalent to example 2, where the bottleneck carrier has no incentive to provide competitive access.

Empirical evidence of widespread cancellations of joint routes on a carrier-specific basis[48] suggests that transactions and information costs of price squeezes are indeed high in the rail industry. There are thousands of commodities moving under countless tariffs over complex route structures. An elaborate system of price squeezes would be required to extract competitors' efficiency gains,[49] but only one letter to the rate bureau or other tariff publishing agent is required to cancel competitive access on all routes. Other limits on the bottleneck carrier's ability to enforce a perfect price squeeze are inflexibilities in revenue divisions, large negotiation costs in changing them, antitrust concerns, and lack of knowledge of relative cost differences. In such circumstances, it is no secret in the rail industry that the bottleneck carrier often can gather almost all the net revenues by simply cancelling competing routes.

Given the cost structure and observed behavior in the rail industry cited above, relying on voluntary negotiations in a regime of imperfect price squeezes thus appears to have severe drawbacks in a transition to deregulation in the rail industry. The carrier with exclusive access is being invited to help itself to all the net revenues on the affected moves, but can do without incurring substantial transactions and information costs only by cancelling all routes regardless of relative efficiency. All net revenues accrue to the cancelling carrier under that action, while that carrier has insufficient incentive to keep open more efficient joint-line routes, not to mention less efficient or equally efficient ones. Meanwhile, the cancellations deny the connecting carrier the ability to compete on a price and service basis and possibly the net revenues it needs for survival. As connecting carriers with a relative deficit of bottlenecks find themselves being squeezed by these route cancellations with little opportunity to retaliate, they in turn will seek merger partners with an aim of creating and taking advantage of additional opportunities to foreclose competition.[50] The likely consequence of the theories supporting a permissive policy toward anticompetitive behavior in a world of large sunk, transactions, and information costs is to make additional (quasi-) rent-seeking rather than efficiency-enhancing vertical mergers highly attractive.

Perhaps it might be argued that transactions and information costs are just other kinds of costs to be encompassed in the efficiency test, which should simply be renegotiated along the newly established welfare frontier (see Figure 2–2 above).[51] According to this logic, the very definition of efficiency means that all beneficial transactions will take place as long as all the costs and benefits (including bounded rationality [Simon 1978] as a cost) are taken into account, thereby justifying the voluntary negotiations approach. If one accepts the conclusion that static efficiency is the only goal of competitive policy, arguments for regulatory intervention would then turn on the possibility that regulatory rules for competitive access may involve fewer transactions costs than voluntary negotiations, thereby facilitating static efficiency gains. Without necessarily accepting such a narrow vision of the public interest in a transition to deregulation in the rail industry, we may now examine this possibility.

THE REVENUE/VARIABLE COST TEST

The previous static efficiency results are so far reciprocal and do not depend on which carrier is given a prior right to the traffic which must be negotiated away by the other carrier before entering the market. If there are zero transactions and information costs as assumed in the permissive model, regulatory restrictions on denial of competitive access will affect the division of the efficiency gains from voluntary negotiations, not the achievement of a static efficient outcome.[52] Nevertheless, the permissive model is cited in opposition to any regulatory interference in the right of the bottleneck carrier to unilaterally deny competitive access because it would purportedly subsidize service by inefficient firms.[53]

But for this to be true, then there must be sufficient transactions and information costs that prevent voluntary negotiations from producing an efficient outcome under the regulatory rule.[54] As we have noted above, however, such transactions and information costs could also bar utilization of a more static efficient joint-line route under the voluntary negotiations approach. Thus a paradox confounds the opposition to regulatory rules promoting competitive access. The only apparent argument that is consistent with the priority of static efficiency departs from the initial rationale: joint-line routes are more likely to be inefficient and should be foreclosed as a general rule by freely applied vertical foreclosures accompanied by high transactions costs of opening up the route to the joint-line carrier.

Given the possibility of vertical foreclosures of more efficient competitors in situations of high transactions costs as discussed above, the objective of regulatory intervention into competitive access issues should be to accomplish "competition on equal terms," but it is unclear precisely how to "levelize the playing field."[55] The major difficulty is the lack of standards for establishing the economically appropriate price of access.

Assuming only the narrow goal of maximizing static efficiency, it seems reasonable to propose four goals for successful regulatory intervention in rail competitive access matters. First, a successful transition to less regulation should be facilitated. Second, the revenue divisions should provide no subsidy to static inefficiency, that is, both carriers should bear any static efficiency losses of holding open a route. Third, strong incentives should motivate the shipper to choose the more static efficient route. Fourth, transactions costs should hopefully be reduced (or not increased materially) by the rule.

The revenue/variable cost (R/VC) test establishes a revenue division for the connecting carrier in competitive access cases such as Figure 3–2[56] to accomplish these objectives such that:

$$\frac{R_{11}}{C'_{11}} = \frac{R_{11} + R_{12}}{C'_{11} + C'_{12}}. \tag{3–15}$$

That is to say, the R/VC test requires that the single-line carrier must hold open the joint route at a division that equates its revenue/variable costs for its single-line and joint-line routes.

In the world of zero transactions, information, and sunk costs assumed in the permissive model, the results of the R/VC test for static efficiency differ little from those discussed above for the case of voluntary negotiations. If the routes are equally efficient, it does not matter which route is used as far as static efficiency is concerned. If the joint-line route is more efficient, the test will affect the division between D_1 and D_2 but not the incentive to use that route. If the single-line route is more efficient, then there will always exist a renegotiation of the division of the efficiency gains from the single-line carrier to the connecting carrier whereby the traffic moves over the more efficient single-line route.[57] A more likely result is that the carriers will offer "allowances" (rebates) to the shipper from their share of the division in the real world of antitrust enforcement, as discussed more fully below.

With the addition of positive sunk costs to the equation, the results of the R/VC test are quite different from reliance on voluntary negotiations.[58] The test prevents the price squeeze that would have appropriated the connecting carrier's sunk costs and therefore makes it more likely that a more static efficient competitor will recover total costs.

With the consideration of positive transactions and information costs, the static efficiency properties of both voluntary negotiations and regulatory intervention do not necessarily hold. Thus it is important to assure that the R/VC test does not subsidize service by inefficient competitors.

Return first to the assumptions of the permissive model that transactions costs may be safely ignored, but assume that sunk costs are important. The R/VC test seeks to achieve the first two objectives above via "competition on equal terms":

1. Both carriers, if equally static efficient, have the same opportunity to price above their incremental costs as is assumed to be necessary to recover sunk and fixed costs on the routes from J to D in Figure 3–2 (no price squeeze by RR_1 is possible, and an equally static efficient connecting carrier receives a revenue division such that its revenue/variable cost is the same as that of the bottleneck carrier), while
2. Both carriers bear 100 percent of any static inefficiency or efficiency created by a decision to compete by holding open their preferred route.[59]

These properties may be readily derived from the test. By definition, when the traffic moves via the joint-line route, the following equations hold:

$$P_2/V_{22} = R_{22} - C'_{22}, \tag{3–16}$$

$$R_{22} = R - R_{11}, \tag{3–17}$$

and by virtue of the R/VC test, we have

$$R_{11} = \left[\frac{R}{C'_{11} + C'_{12}} \right] C'_{11}. \tag{3–18}$$

Therefore, by substitution, we have

$$P_2/V_{22} = \left[\frac{R}{C'_{11} + C'_{12}} \right] C'_{12} - C'_{12} - [C'_{22} - C'_{12}]. \tag{3–19}$$

Equation 3–19 may be interpreted as follows. The first difference on the right-hand side is between the unit incremental revenue and cost that the bottleneck carrier would have received under the rule if the traffic moved single-line rather than joint-line. Under the rule, the connecting carrier receives this same net revenue for its portion of the movement plus an additional sum equal to its static efficiency advantage (disadvantage), which is the last term in brackets. When both carriers are equally efficient, the last term is zero and both carriers earn the same revenue/variable cost for their movements and have an equal opportunity to price above incremental cost in order to recover sunk costs. The first two terms in equation 3–19 thus satisfy the first objective above.

Whenever the single-line route is more efficient, the adverse static efficiency consequences from allowing the shipper to choose the joint-line route create an adverse profit variance which is borne entirely by the connecting carrier that elected to hold open the route. The last term in brackets thus satisfies the second objective of competition on equal terms.

The same efficiency result may be shown in terms of ratios rather than absolute dollars.[60] Assume the single-line movement is the more static efficient. The greater efficiency of the single-line route will produce a higher R/VC than for the joint-line route, and by virtue of the R/VC test we have:

$$\frac{R_{11}}{C'_{11}} = \frac{R_{11} + R_{12}}{C'_{11} + C'_{12}} > \frac{R_{11} + R_{22}}{C'_{11} + C'_{22}}. \qquad (3\text{–}20)$$

We know that the R/VC of the joint-line route is a weighted average of the R/VC of the two routes, where the weights are the respective shares of the total variable cost of the joint-line route:

$$\frac{R_{11} + R_{22}}{C'_{11} + C'_{22}} = \left[\frac{C'_{11}}{C'_{11} + C'_{22}}\right]\left[\frac{R_{11}}{C'_{11}}\right] + \left[\frac{C'_{22}}{C'_{11} + C'_{22}}\right]\left[\frac{R_{22}}{C'_{22}}\right]. \qquad (3\text{–}21)$$

Then it must be true that

$$\frac{R_{11} + R_{12}}{C'_{11} + C'_{12}} = \frac{R_{11}}{C'_{11}} > \frac{R_{22}}{C'_{22}}, \qquad (3\text{–}22)$$

since equation 3–17 holds and the weights sum to one. Whenever the joint-line route is less efficient than the single-line route, the decline in the R/VC for the through movement from using the less efficient route is borne entirely by a decline in the connecting carrier's R/VC. Conversely, the inequalities are reversed when the single-line route is less efficient and the difference in R/VC between the routes is borne by the single-line carrier.

This property of the rule permits examination of the incentives for static efficiency via the third objective identified above. This objective is accomplished by allowing price competition by each carrier to offer inducements to the shipper to choose the route it prefers under the rule.[61] Starting with R_{22} as established by the R/VC rule on the joint-line route, the maximum "allowance" that the connecting carrier can offer to the shipper to encourage the joint-line route is its net revenues on the route, $R_{22} - C'_{22}$. The maximum allowance that the bottleneck carrier can offer to encourage the single-line route is the increase in its net revenues when the traffic moves over the single-line route, $R_{22} - C'_{12}$. Obviously, when $C'_{12} < C'_{22}$, the single-line carrier can always outbid the connecting carrier (and conversely when the connecting carrier is the more efficient). The greater the static efficiency differences and thus concern over choosing an inefficient route, the easier it will be for the more efficient carrier to undercut the other's price offer to the shipper.[62]

These static efficiency properties of the R/VC test may be illustrated by means of Table 3–3, which computes the results of applying the test to the previous examples in Figure 3–4. The principle of competition on equal terms is first illustrated by reference to example 3, where the carriers are equally efficient. There both carriers achieve the same ability to price above incremental cost to recover sunk costs (the R/VC is the same for both).

The second feature of the competition on equal terms test is illustrated by comparing examples 1 and 2 with example 3. When the connecting carrier has a $2 cost advantage, its net revenues increase by that amount (compare example 1 with example 3 for carrier *B*) for the joint-line route. In the second example, the connecting carrier's net revenues decrease by exactly the amount of its cost disadvantage (compare example 2 with example 3 for carrier *B*) for the joint-line route.

Note that this same principle may be expressed as R/VC ratios as shown in equation 3–21. For example, the R/VC of the joint-line route is the weighted average of the R/VC of the two carrier's routes. Note also that the single-line carrier earns incremental net revenues of $5 for completing the entire haul, but the more efficient connecting carrier earns an additional $2 (its efficiency advantage) in example 1.

These static efficiency properties of the R/VC test do not explicitly consider possible transactions costs under the rule. To achieve these efficiency results, the rule should achieve the fourth objective of reducing the transactions costs which are the obstacle to efficiency under voluntary negotiations. The R/VC test seeks this result by automatically conferring the benefits of a static cost advantage on the competitive link to the carrier responsible for the efficiency. No transactions costs are incurred with the

Table 3–3
Net Revenues and Revenue/Variable Costs of Alternative Routes in Hypothetical Examples: Revenue/Variable Cost Test

Carrier	Single-Line Route: Net Revenues	Single-Line Route: Revenue/Variable Cost	Joint-Line Route: Net Revenues	Joint-Line Route: Revenue/Variable Cost
		Example 1		
A	$10	2.0	$ 5	2.0
B	0	--	7	3.3
Total	$10	2.0	$12	2.5
		Example 2		
A	$10	2.0	$ 5	2.0
B	0	--	4	1.7
Total	$10	2.0	$ 9	1.81
		Example 3		
A	$10	2.0	$ 5	2.0
B	0	--	5	2.0
Total	$10	2.0	$10	2.0

Source: Figure 3-4

rule such as when the bottleneck carrier appropriates the connecting carrier's efficiency gains under the theory of voluntary negotiations.

The R/VC test may be interpreted in Figure 3–3 as a division of the revenues such that point E is automatically achieved when $D_1 + D_2 > 0$ and point F when $D_1 + D_2 < 0$. The efficiency gains go automatically to the carrier responsible for opening up a more efficient route. When $D_1 + D_2 = 0$, there is no efficiency gain to be allocated. Note that points E and F are entirely symmetric and give concrete meaning to the second objective of competition on equal terms. The test does not create an asymmetry where the connecting carrier has to forfeit most of its static efficiency advantages as the price of entry while allowing the single-line carrier to keep its static efficiency gains entirely.[63]

Net gains in static efficiency are more likely to be achieved under the rule if information costs are low—carriers' relative costs are well known. Under such circumstances the transactions costs of enforcing the rule are likely to be low (the results of the rule will be predictable because incremental costs will be known by all) and possible incentives for "gaming the rules" will be lessened.[64] But even if regulatory costs under the rule equate to transactions costs under the theory of voluntary negotiations, the goal of a successful transition to deregulation is enhanced via price competition and the connecting carrier's recovery of its sunk costs.[65]

Despite these incentives for static efficiency, it is true that there is nothing about the R/VC test that ensures that shippers will always choose the most static efficient route. Indeed, making the movement of traffic over the most static efficient route the only determinant of policy produces rather peculiar recommendations for rail competitive access in a transition to deregulation. If the carriers have the same incremental costs, the connecting carrier is forced out of business by the denial of access, but the loss of competition is judged to be of little concern.[66] Likewise, if one carrier has a cost disadvantage, that route[67] is forced to exit the market, and all the traffic goes to the other route. Making static efficiency in routing traffic the only goal in establishing competitive access policy results in the conclusion that competition is redundant when the conditions for a competitive equilibrium of equally efficient firms are satisfied and possibly harmful when it is not. Such a limited goal would hardly be the recipe for a successful transition to deregulation in an industry with substantial sunk costs.

The merits of regulatory intervention into rail competitive access disputes do not depend on assuming that the bottleneck carrier will otherwise act contrary to its self-interest, as the rationale for the permissive approach claims. Nor is a benefit of the revenue/variable cost test that static efficiency can be guaranteed in a regime of positive sunk, transactions, and information costs. Rather the merits are seen by reference to the previously listed objectives of competitive access policy: (1) the carrier possessing the bottleneck cannot use control of competitive access to appropriate a competitor's sunk costs and efficiency gains, thus enhancing the likelihood of a competitive market in the longer run and a successful transition to deregulation; (2) no static inefficient carrier (either the single-line or joint-line carrier) holds open a route without being forced to absorb fully the costs of its relative inefficiency (but is free to do so if it chooses[68]); (3) both carriers are free to engage in price competition (via "allowances," i.e., rebates from the filed rate), and the more static efficient carrier can always undercut the price of the less static efficient firm; and (4) transactions costs are likely to be lowered relative to the voluntary negotiations model.

THE REVENUE ADEQUACY OBJECTION

In addition to static efficiency concerns in the rail industry, other objections to policies designed to promote competitive access have emerged: (1) concerns that intramodal competition leads to what used to be called "destructive competition" for the rail industry and should be foreclosed by carriers with market power,[69] and (2) a belief that carriers with exclusive access should be encouraged to apply a "price squeeze" on the connecting carrier to capture all the net revenues regardless of which route is the most static efficient.[70] Both of these amount to preferences for a particular distribution of net income among firms, not static efficiency considerations. An additional concern is that the intramodal competition that results from open competitive access would foreclose the single-line carrier's ability to implement Ramsey pricing.[71]

Th distribution of net income for the traffic between the two carriers was initially treated as a matter of indifference in the static efficiency rationale for a permissive policy on denied competitive access. But as static efficiency concerns are shown to militate against the permissive model, determination of the distribution of the net income becomes more central to competitive access issues. Opponents of regulatory actions to promote competitive access reach their conclusions on the optimum distribution of net revenues between the single-line and connecting carrier by first defining the achievement of revenue adequacy of incumbent carriers as the central objective of regulators, even in a deregulated world.[72] The revenue adequacy problem then is considered entirely from the point of view of the bottleneck carrier.[73]

The weakness of this version of the revenue-adequacy concern in a regime of deregulation is rather obvious. The single-line carrier is improving its revenue adequacy only by foreclosing the connecting carrier's ability to survive by causing a deterioration in its revenue adequacy. The permissive theory is arguing that all the net revenues should go to the carrier willing to use its exclusive access to foreclose competition or apply a price squeeze. The R/VC test, as shown above, permits both carriers to retain their efficiency advantages and achieve revenues above variable costs believed needed for both carriers to be revenue adequate. If the principal consideration is revenue adequacy in an industry where the majority of movements are joint-line, the problem must be addressed at the level of the industry, not the self-interest of bottleneck firms in having the revenue-adequacy problem solved only for themselves.[74] At this level, the facts that all carriers have a similar revenue-adequacy problem and must price above variable costs to recover sunk costs are crucial.[75]

Opponents object to the R/VC ratio test because it permits price competition that might possibly drive rail rates down to variable cost on the competitive links.[76] According to the theory, achieving revenue adequacy should be the principal goal of regulators in the rail industry, and the connecting carrier will be forced by competition to rebate these net revenues to the shipper. Using rules for competitive access to achieve competition on equal terms will allegedly eliminate the bottleneck carrier's ability to practice the Ramsey pricing believed necessary for revenue adequacy. The theory states that it is better to allow the bottleneck carrier to appropriate the connecting carrier's net revenues to achieve revenue adequacy rather than let the shipper get them.

But a desire to suppress price competition is a questionable principal guiding force for competitive access policy during a transition to deregulation. Further, the objection to procompetitive access policies in the rail industry on the grounds that they produce intramodal price competition that impedes achievement of Ramsey efficient prices points to an additional difficulty with the permissive model's vision of a deregulated equilibrium in the rail industry. The presence of large sunk and fixed costs is said to require Ramsey prices well in excess of incremental costs.[77] According to the theory, direct intramodal competition drives rail rates to incremental costs.[78] The theory also states that carriers will establish the necessary Ramsey prices freely without regulatory intervention[79] and that an equilibrium of competitors operating under conditions of increasing returns and establishing revenue-adequate Ramsey prices well in excess of incremental costs is a sustainable equilibrium in a contestable deregulated transportation market.[80] The theory also states that price must equal and cannot exceed marginal cost in a contestable market occupied by more than one incumbent.[81]

This raises the possibility of a discrepancy between (1) the vision of a deregulated rail industry composed of competing firms practicing Ramsey pricing with (2) the opposition to intramodal competition on the grounds that it is ruinous given the assumed cost structure. If one characterizes procompetitive access policies as an effort to move rail markets as close as possible to the contestable ideal ("a surrogate for competition unimpeded by entry barriers"), it would appear that the objective of pursuing perfectly contestable markets as the welfare-maximizing ideal could conflict with the pursuit of welfare gains through Ramsey pricing. These difficulties in the permissive approach to competitive access reflect difficulties in the larger scheme for a deregulated rail industry and call for a more detailed examination of the fundamental assumptions behind a "competitive market model" of competing firms practicing Ramsey pricing in highly contestable markets and operating under multiproduct scale economies in Chapter 4.

CONCLUSION

The permissive approach toward vertical foreclosures contains logical difficulties and fails to explain observed behavior in the rail industry. Nevertheless, it has become the rationale for an extremely permissive approach by the ICC toward denials of competitive access in the rail industry. These permissive attitudes have profound implications for achieving a successful transition to deregulation in the rail industry. Introducing the effects of sunk, transactions, and information costs into the model radically alters the conclusions, better explains observed behavior, and leads to recommendations for policies on competitive access that improve the chances for a successful transition to deregulation while preserving incentives for achievement of static efficiency gains.

As in Chapter 2, a common response to these paradoxes is to disbelieve that a logically integrated body of theory such as that of contestable markets could actually lead to such odd results in practical applications of the theory. Perhaps the applications of the theory have been misrepresented or misinterpreted, or perhaps the logical difficulties in the applications can be tidied up by dropping inconsistent claims for the theory.

However, the logical difficulties of the permissive model towards vertical foreclosure are not so easily resolved. Applications of the model encounter these paradoxes not because of a failure of logical thinking, but because application of contestability theory creates extreme assumptions where the ambivalence of the entire literature on vertical foreclosure may be seen with greater clarity. This literature claims that restrictive vertical market practices have substantial potential for efficiency gains,[82] yet cautions that antitrust authorities must nevertheless be vigilant to prevent anticompetitive abuses.[83] While the literature often embraces one or the other extreme explanation, contestability theory provides the idealized market environment where the two explanations for restrictive vertical practices are seen to arise from the same types of market imperfections, at least for the case at hand.

The crucial role of transactions costs in evaluating efficiency gains and anticompetitive consequences of restrictive practices in vertical economic relationships was recognized long before contestability theory was offered as a "unifying analytical structure" for resolving antitrust concerns. The potential anticompetitive consequences previously identified in the transactions costs approach, however, were generally limited to strategic purposes and enhanced oligopolistic interaction.[84]

The explicit consideration of transactions and sunk costs clarifies difficult paradoxes regarding the current permissive approach toward vertical foreclosures both in economics and, to a much lesser degree, in the law.[85] Such practices are widely believed to (1) achieve important efficiency gains while (2) not risking anticompetitive behavior. The analysis here shows that the market imperfections that are to be corrected via the vertical foreclosure to achieve the alleged efficiency gains must be narrowly enough circumscribed to prevent incentives to engage in the alleged anticompetitive behavior. Clearly this has not yet been possible in recent reliance on the permissive model to bless vertical foreclosures in the rail industry.

Initially, objections to regulatory intervention to enhance competitive access focused on static efficiency concerns. After it became clear that such concerns were based on inconsistent assumptions regarding the role of transactions costs and a failure to consider the role of sunk costs in the transition to deregulation, the debate turned to an alleged conflict between the need for Ramsey pricing to achieve adequate revenues and procompetitive access policies. Such claims require a reexamination of the role of price discrimination in highly contestable markets. The next chapter shows that movements to perfect contestability do in fact produce a "market meltdown" where Ramsey pricing schemes cannot be sustained among incumbents in the same market. The complete reliance by contestability theory on potential entry as the answer to possible anticompetitive concerns thus raises serious questions regarding the broad claims for a permissive approach based on the theory.

NOTES

1. See Chapter 1 above for discussion.
2. See Posner (1978–1979). For a reply, see Louis Kaplow (1985).
3. "Transactions costs" are the administrative and legal costs of negotiating and policing sales agreements. See Alchian and Allen (1968). The assumption that transactions and information costs are zero is implicit in the conventional theory justifying a permissive approach to vertical foreclosure. See, for example, McFarland (1987) and Marshall and Cook (1986). As will be shown below, zero transactions costs and perfect information are crucial to the conclusions of the permissive approach to vertical foreclosure.
4. Contestability analysis allows for a circumstance where costs are fixed but not sunk, the case of the "contestable monopoly." See Baumol and Willig (1981).
5. See Coase (1960). The paradox is that the permissive model of vertical foreclosure assumes that static efficiency is the only goal and that the permissive model will always produce an efficient result. But other initial endowments of bargaining power will also produce that result (at least in the short-term, static, perfect information, and zero transactions cost models employed in this analysis).

If one is indifferent to the consequences for income distribution and willing to assume perfect information and no transactions costs to negotiations, any arbitrary market structure (even natural monopoly) can be shown to result in an efficient outcome in a narrow, short-term economic welfare sense. See Posner (1969). The welfare properties of the endowment of net income and its dynamic effects on concentration and competition, not short-run efficiency considerations, then paradoxically become the only consideration in the choice between alternatives. See also Dewey (1974).

6. Baumol (1986b) notes that markets and contracts will not automatically achieve efficiency and call for transactions cost analysis under circumstances of "asset specificity (sunk costs), limits on information and calculation ability ('bounded rationality'), and willingness to profit at the expense of others ('opportunism')." All three seem to be important in the rail industry. The results of this chapter may be thought of as supportive of the idea that even small sunk costs can have major effects on the competitive equilibrium and economic welfare and must be explicitly accounted for. See Schwartz and Reynolds (1983) and Stiglitz (1987).

7. As discussed in Chapter 1, "the unifying analytical structure" of contestability "aspire[s] to provide no less than a unifying theory for the analysis of industrial organization" to replace the theory of perfect competition. See Baumol, Panzar, and Willig (1982, 320–321) and Baumol (1982, 1–2, 15). The theory of contestable markets is offered as a "competitive market model" to be used as a guide to regulators when they seek to serve as "surrogates for competition" in the transition to deregulation for regulated industries.

8. See Collins (1985) and Wheeler and Frieland (1986). In its own words, the ICC's standards have been "liberal" and "have allowed cancellation of joint rates in almost all situations." See *Ex Parte* No. 445, "Standards for Intramodal Competition," *Decision*, 7 July 1983, 10. See *Federal Register*, 48, no. 133 (11 July 1983): 31, 672–31, 677. See also ICC, *Ex Parte* No. 427, "Joint Rates Study—Report to Congress," served 17 March 1982, Docket no. 39176 (Sub-no. 1), *Pittsburgh & Lake Erie Railroad Co.* v. *Consolidated Rail Corp.* (decision served 9 April 1985); *Restructured Rates on Grain and Grain Products—Conrail*, 365 ICC 635 (1982); *Joint Line Cancellation—Soda Ash—UPR Co.*, 365 ICC 951 (1982); *Interchange Provisions at Jacksonville, FL, SCL and SRS*, 365 ICC 905 (1982); *Investigation & Suspension* no. 9258, *Routing Between Stations—Conrail*—November 1982; Docket no. 38676, *Change in Routing Provisions—Conrail*—July 1981, 365 ICC 753; and *Midtec Paper Corp. et al.* v. *Chicago and Northwestern Transportation Company*, served 17 July 1985.

9. Tye (1986c), Grimm and Harris (1983), Grimm (1984a, 1984b), and Brand and Leckie (1984).

10. More generally, in the antitrust field these issues have been addressed in the context of "essential facility," "bottleneck," "price squeeze," "vertical foreclosures," "tying," "dual distribution," and other related law of vertical competitive relationships. See U.S. Department of Justice (1985) and The National Association of Attorneys General (1985). For an economic review of these issues, see Scherer (1980) and Tye (1987d). For a review of some of the legal issues, see Troy (1983). Some of the more pertinent legal precedents are *Otter Tail Power Co.* v. *United States*, 410 U.S. 366 (1973); *Mt. Hood Stages, Inc.* v. *Greyhound*, 535 F.2d 687 (9th Circuit, 1977); *United States* v. *Aluminum Company of America*, 148 F.2d 416

(2nd Circuit, 1945); *Brown Shoe Co., Inc.* v. *United States*, 370 U.S. 294 (1962); and *United States* v. *Terminal Railroad Association of St. Louis*, 224 U.S. 383 (1912).

11. For the exposition of the theory of voluntary negotiations, see the ICC's reasoning in the Rulemaking on DT&I Conditions, 366 ICC 112 (1982), and at 367 ICC 753–54, 444 (1983), in *Exemption from Regulation—Boxcar Traffic*. For support for the Commission's theory, see Baumol and Willig (1985a, 1985b) and Willig (1984b). For applications of these principles to postmerger reductions in rail competition and trackage rights, see Baumol (1983a, 1984a, 1984b, 1986a).

12. See Baumol (1984b, Tr. 10,084).

13. Bailey and Baumol (1984, 123, 124, 137).

14. *Chesapeake and Ohio* v. *ICC*, 704 F.2d 373 (7th Circuit, 1983).

15. U.S. General Accounting Office (1987) reports a survey where the principal explanation cited for cancellation of competitive access by the defendant carriers was retaliation for previous vertical foreclosures, not the pursuit of efficiency gains. Railroads generally refer to one another as "friendly" or "unfriendly" connections, not "efficient" or "inefficient." See also Cook (1987, 48):

> Once deregulation took hold in the early Eighties, the railroads began repudiating the joint rates, through routes and reciprocal switching agreements that had traditionally eased the flow of traffic from one line to another. Instead, they tried to control every ton of traffic they could by offering single-line service between shipper and customer *even if, in stiff-arming another line, it involved moving traffic longer distances* [emphasis added].

16. See Ordover and Willig (1983, 571):

> The literature . . . leads to some challenging conclusions that conform with some of the conclusions reached by the "old" learning in industrial organization and antitrust. In particular, *the new research generally agrees on one principle: that vertical conduct by a firm with a protected dominant market position cannot rationally be presumed to be in the public interest*. Rather, such prevalent elements of economic structure as inferior sources of supply (or complementary products), diverse consumer tastes, price inflexibilities, and rate of return constraints can lead to incentives for anticompetitive vertical conduct, such as exclusionary vertical mergers [emphasis added].

See also Warren-Boulton (1978), Blair and Kaserman (1983), Williamson (1975), and Krattenmaker and Salop (1986).

17. See Chapter 2 and detailed discussion below. In a perfect price squeeze, the firm controlling competitive access establishes a price of access slightly above the marginal costs of a more efficient unintegrated competitor, thereby appropriating any efficiency gain from entry and creating a profit motive for granting competitive access.

18. Ordover, Sykes, and Willig (1985).

19. The notation in this chapter is self-contained and does not refer to Chapter 2.

20. Carriers must agree on a "through route" through the junction (i.e., a joint service agreement) for the traffic to physically move. The bottleneck carrier must

agree on a "joint rate" from *O* to *D* or publish a "proportional" rate from *O* to *J* as well.

21. Note that R_{11} and R_{12} are undefined in the absence of a joint route and revenue division agreement between the carriers, for example, a "vertical foreclosure." The issue to be decided is whether such prices should be established voluntarily or whether intervention by regulators is required.

22. Assuming that costs are both fixed and sunk allows a focus on the crucial role of zero sunk costs in the argument for a permissive approach to competitive access in the rail industry.

23. The rail industry is to be subject to both substantial sunk and fixed costs. Therefore it is commonly assumed that both carriers in competitive access proceedings need to price above marginal, variable, and incremental costs in order to be revenue adequate. See Baumol (1983b; 1985b, 25–26, 36). Variable costs are usually used as proxies for marginal costs and incremental costs. See Baumol and Willig (1985d, 22–25; 1985c, 25, 27–29), where the "incremental costs" used in measuring efficiency across routes is equated to the "variable costs" which must be exceeded for revenue adequacy. See also Willig (1984b, 12), where the "minimum costs" relevant to static efficiency concerns in competitive access cases is defined as "going concern value." Section 201 of the *Staggers Rail Act* defined pricing at the "going concern value" as a rate that "equals or exceeds the variable costs of the transportation," where "the commission may not include in such variable costs expense that does not vary directly with the level of transportation provided." The ICC has defined variability for going concern value to be relatively short run. See ICC Decision in *Ex Parte* No. 335, *Cost Standards for Railroad Rates*, served 9 July 1980.

24. In connection with its regulatory responsibilities, the ICC has developed a standard methodology and data (disputed, of course, in individual rate proceedings) for estimation of variable costs. For further discussion of its uses, see Tye (1984b).

25. "Static efficiency" in this context refers to cost comparisons based on "variable costs" of the traffic on alternative routes and is the measure of economic welfare by proponents of a permissive approach to problems in discussions of railroad competitive access. See Willig (1984b, 9):

> The Commission's regulatory role in this area [competitive access] can and should be limited to ensuring that a railroad with market power does not use that power to divert traffic to a less efficient route.

See also Baumol and Willig (1985c, 9). The static efficiency measure of course ignores dynamic (long-term) welfare gains and losses and does not consider downstream welfare gains and losses resulting from the effect of the restrictive vertical practice on prices. (Volume is assumed constant.) Considering only static welfare gains or losses on the production side thus elides all the issues arising over whether a particular vertical practice will cause downstream prices to rise or fall. See Westfield (1981), who states that "the results are not easily summarized." The static measure of welfare gain and loss will nevertheless be accepted for the initial purpose of examining the logic of the permissive model, but it will be questioned below. Of course, actual routing decisions should be based on total logistics cost and service differences. These could be added to the analysis to increase the generality of the results without affecting the basic conclusions.

26. Baumol and Willig (1985b, 26), state that "it will always be possible . . . to offer a sufficiently attractive price (i.e., a competitive price)" to the connecting carrier. See also Tye (1987c) and McFarland (1987) for hypothetical examples of the pricing mechanism.

27. Under the assumptions of contestability theory, the threat of entry alone is sufficient to achieve the optimum welfare properties of the model. No additional positive role is assigned to actual competition rather than potential competition.

28. See Baumol (1982). Departures from contestability are discussed below.

29. Note that this figure is conceptually similar to Figure 2–2, except the latter includes positive transactions costs.

30. A price squeeze is not simply an incidental or unintended consequence of the application of the voluntary negotiations theory to the rail industry competitive access problem. Such negotiations work to eliminate rail routing inefficiency according to the theory only if the price squeeze on the connecting carrier is "perfect" or sufficiently so. See Ordover, Sykes, and Willig (1985).

31. For development of the parity principle, see Baumol (1984a) and Willig (1979a).

32. Put another way, (1) the connecting carrier is unable unilaterally to offer a price inducement to the shipper to choose a more efficient joint-line route because its revenue division was already established by the bottleneck carrier at the minimum level necessary to induce entry and appropriate for itself the efficiency gains from entry, and (2) the potential for entry by the connecting carrier in no way undermines the bottleneck carrier's ability to exploit the lack of contestability on the bottleneck.

33. An example frequently cited is the "DT&I Conditions," whereby a railroad was required to keep open routes with nonvertically integrated competitors after a vertical merger. See Tye (1987b).

34. As shown below, forcing the single-line carrier to give up its efficiency gains to the connecting carrier when the price of access is established would affect the division of the efficiency gain (D_1 and D_2) but not the static efficiency results. Such preferences for the connecting carrier are not as far-fetched as they may sound to someone unfamiliar with the rail industry. They are called "preferential solicitation agreements," and may have been imposed by regulators as a condition for approving a merger.

35. See Baumol and Willig (1985b, 18). The need for a refusal to deal to foreclose inefficient competitors may be thought of as a claim that the single-line carrier possesses a multiproduct natural monopoly (i.e., its use lowers total industry costs) which is price unsustainable. See Panzar and Willig (1977). This claim of a price unsustainable natural monopoly is contrary to proposition 1, that a perfect price squeeze is always available to achieve the efficient outcome via voluntary negotiations.

36. No one doubts that fixed and sunk costs in the railroad industry are as great as found anywhere in American industry. The ICC has estimated that "revenue adequacy" in the rail industry as a whole would require rates on average of about 152 percent of variable costs. See Tye (1984a). Such fixed costs are also sunk for extremely long periods as well.

37. See Goldberg (1976).

38. Perhaps the connecting carrier might improve its position by engaging in

"strategic behavior," that is, refusing to deal to force a better share of the benefits of its greater efficiency. Such behavior would depart from the zero transactions cost assumption as well as the permissive model's denial that voluntary negotiations would produce static inefficiency and denial of any role for oligopolistic behavior. See Baumol (1982, 2). In any event, the connecting firm's credibility is weakened by its poor bargaining position and it is certainly the case that the model does not assure the long-run survival of a more static efficient connecting carrier.

39. Put in the language of contestability, if the bottleneck carrier is to deal with the connecting carrier on a "neutral basis," there must be no exit costs for the bottleneck carrier when it chooses to route the traffic via a more static efficient connecting carrier. If both carriers have in fact sunk their costs, the only way the bottleneck carrier can be motivated voluntarily to exit the market is by appropriating for itself the revenues that the more static efficient connecting carrier needs to amortize its sunk costs.

40. The price squeeze does not meet the economist's narrow definition of "predatory" because it imposes a cost on the competitor at no loss to the squeezing carrier. Predation, as defined by economists, usually assumes some at least temporary cost to the predator.

41. The price squeeze creates a cross-subsidy because the resulting allocation of revenues will violate the Stand-Alone Cost test.

42. See note 5 above.

43. See Baumol and Willig (1985c, 45–46; 1986b).

44. For the rationale why the price squeeze must be applied in the permissive model—to create an incentive for the bottleneck carrier voluntarily to pursue the achievement of static efficienty—see Baumol and Willig (1985b, 23).

45. We skip over case 3 in Figure 3–1 as uninteresting for the rail industry.

46. The existence of information and calculation costs associated with the pursuit of optimizing behavior is often referred to as a condition of "bounded rationality." See Simon (1978). In the present case, information costs are incurred in acquiring information about relative operating efficiencies and knowledge of the other carrier's bargaining strategy. Information may be combined with transactions costs for the purposes at hand to identify costs of the transaction in addition to the operating costs of the connecting carrier.

47. For a treatment of the role of transactions and information costs in resale price maintenance, see Rey and Tirole (1986).

48. See above-cited literature and Judge Posner's cited decision. The fact that carriers themselves claim that a foreclosure was necessary to achieve static efficiency itself is consistent with the idea that transactions and information costs of the price squeeze were so high as to preclude the voluntary negotiations model from working.

49. In the author's experience, many railroad executives do not understand the theory supporting the voluntary negotiations model even after hours of discussion, much less apply it. This suggests "bounded rationality" (Simon 1978) as one possible explanation source of high information and transactions costs in the industry.

50. See Ordover and Willig (1983, 571). The resulting increase in size also gives the carrier further clout to retaliate and thus acts as a deterrent against other firms' actions to foreclose the merged firm's own competitive access.

51. See also Baumol and Willig (1985c, 57).

52. The ICC has eliminated the "DT&I Conditions," which routinely required

merged rail carriers to keep open routes and divisions prevailing prior to the merger. See Tye (1986b). At the same time, it has also taken an extremely permissive approach toward vertical foreclosures. But if it believed the assumptions of that model, it could simply rely on voluntary negotiations to eliminate any inefficient services provided for under the DT&I conditions.

53. Baumol and Willig (1985c, 2) characterized the revenue/variable cost test discussed below as "a blatantly protectionist device" which would constitute a "permanent subsidy." See also McFarland (1987).

54. With zero transactions and information costs, the affected carriers will simply pursue voluntary negotiations to eliminate any efficiencies arising from the rule.

55. "Competition on equal terms" has not been given a clear meaning in the vertical foreclosure literature. In *United States* v. *American Telephone and Tel. Co.*, 524 F.Supp. 1360 (D.C. Circuit, 1981), the Court stated that competitive access must be afforded:

> upon such just and reasonable terms and regulations as will, in respect of use, character and cost of services, place every such company upon nearly an equal plane as may be. [footnote omitted]

United States v. *Terminal R.R. Asssociation*, supra, 224 U.S. at 411, 32 S. Ct. at 515.

56. Figure 3–2 illustrates the so-called "rat tail" problem. The more general case of gateway cancellations involves "short hauling" where neither carrier has a single-line route capable of serving the entire journey. Examples of these cases involve the "two-tailed rat" or parallelogram-type route structures. Many such cases will be settled by private negotiations since neither carrier can unilaterally foreclose the other. In such cases where regulatory intervention is nevertheless called for, a variant of the R/VC test could be used. Making the R/VC ratio of the short-hauled carrier equal to that of the most efficient joint-line route in these circumstances would have the static efficiency properties described below for the case of the "rat tail."

57. With zero transactions and information costs, the single-line carrier will be able to share with the connecting carrier the efficiency gains of diverting traffic to the single-line route.

58. Note, however, that opening up competitive access can subvert prior regulatory agreements for recovery of sunk costs as well as preserve the prior agreements. The R/VC test is therefore not offered as a general solution to the competitive access problem. This calls for a "rule of reason" application of these principles across industries. See Tye (1987d).

59. The R/VC rule may be thought of as one way of achieving Quirmbach's (1982) objective of ensuring that vertical integration is socially beneficial in the case where one or more of the firms is not contestable by making a stipulation "as a condition of integration that the external price [R_{11} in the above example] remain fixed [after a vertical merger] and that all intermediate demand at that price be met."

60. Baumol and Willig (1985b, 20) state that "the ratio of a railroad's revenues to its variable cost along a particular route has no connection with its relative efficiency in serving that route."

61. Under the Staggers Act, carriers are not required to charge the published

tariff, but may offer "allowances." Such rebates are commonplace, and often involve confidential contracts designed to encourage the shipper to choose a preferred route.

62. Baumol and Willig (1985c, 6) state that the revenue/variable cost test "would effectively undermine the competitive process while marching under the banner of competition" and would "offer [the connecting carrier] protected enclaves in which regulation immunizes them from effective competition by single line routes." See Tye (1989) for a more complete examination of incentives under the test.

63. Thus the test also enhances prospects for enhanced dynamic efficiency in the longer run, which would be blunted by a scheme that allowed one carrier to appropriate for itself the benefits of another carrier's innovations as the price of competitive access.

64. Critics assert that the carriers will seek to "game" the regulatory process rather than compete under the rule. For example, the bottleneck carrier might seek to inflate its variable costs and content itself with maximizing its revenues on the joint-line route rather than to compete to divert traffic to the single-line route. The ability to do so would represent a departure from the contestability model assumption of perfect information. Nevertheless, it does raise issues of implementation of the rule addressed in Tye (1989).

65. Of course, it might be argued that the R/VC rule would increase regulatory costs while reducing transactions costs, thus not necessarily leading to net welfare gains. However, a case can be made that such a comprehensive weighting of costs and benefits would also militate in favor of the rule. The welfare gains of promoting a successful transition to deregulation are likely to swamp any difference between increased regulatory costs and reduced transactions costs. Such rules on access are meant to be transitory as long-term contracts between carriers replace regulation in the transition to deregulation. See Meyer and Tye (1988). And an explicit regulatory rule for competitive access, such as the R/VC test, is likely to decrease litigation costs considerably compared to a policy of simply "muddling through," because regulatory actions will be more predictable. See Tye (1987c). Finally, as discussed below, constraints on opportunistic behavior by rail carriers are a signal from regulators that revenue adequacy concerns during the transition to deregulation must be addressed by the pursuit of true efficiency gains, not vertical foreclosures to achieve "rent-seeking" objectives at the expense of other carriers.

66. As noted above, in contestability analysis actual competition among incumbents has no welfare significance in the presence of hit-and-run entry.

67. Note that it is the bottleneck carrier's route that exits the market when it is less efficient. For the connecting carrier, the route and the carrier are both shut down in the relevant market.

68. One of the reasons it may wish to absorb this static inefficiency is that it may have a long-run efficiency advantage in sunk costs that more than offsets its static inefficiency in variable costs. This possibility is one more weakness of making static efficiency the only goal of procompetitive access and then permitting the bottleneck carrier to foreclose competition.

69. See Baumol (1985a).

70. See Baumol and Willig (1985b, 1985c).

71. See Baumol and Willig (1985b, 23–24). If the revenue/variable cost test were adopted, one possible consequence would be that the single-line carrier would be

forced to compete for the traffic. As a result of this competition, it would "have to forego much or all of its right to differential pricing, driving rates below efficient market levels." The U.S. Department of Transportation (1985) opposed competitive access on similar grounds. The resulting competition, it alleged, "could *thereby bring the entire joint rate structure down* to the lowest rate-to-cost ratio prevailing on any route without regard to competitive circumstances, *revenue need*, or the public interest" [emphasis added].

72. "Adequacy of revenues is the fundamental and overriding necessary condition for economic efficiency. . . . It is appropriate to do *anything* which achieves adequate revenues as quickly as possible" [emphasis added]. See Baumol and Willig (1983b, 26).

73. The problems with this objection are best illustrated by the objection that the R/VC test will create a situation where

> the connecting railroad could earn a far more substantial contribution from its portion of that route . . . in a case where the carrier with exclusive access is the unfortunate possessor of a high-cost alternative single-line route.

See Baumol and Willig (1985c, 26). Surely it is not consistent to claim that the R/VC test is an irrelevant measure of efficiency while also expressing concern for the plight of the less efficient single-line carrier precisely because it must necessarily bear the cost of its inefficiency under the rule.

74. The revenue adequacy problem must be defined from the industry point of view, not from that of an individual firm. See Damus (1984), Spencer and Brander (1983), and McFarland (1986).

75. Regulatory rules to prevent vertical foreclosures of competition, such as the R/VC test, are a powerful means for regulators to communicate to firms undergoing a transition to deregulation that they must solve their revenue adequacy problems under regulation with true efficiency gains, not "rent-seeking behavior." These efficiency gains from a successful transition to deregulation are likely to swamp all the concerns over static operating efficiency, transactions costs, and so forth. See Meyer and Tye (1985, 1988).

76. Note that this price competition arises because of the decision to eliminate regulatory standards for minimum prices (the previous method of enhancing ability to recover sunk costs) as part of regulatory reform.

77. Baumol and Willig (1983a, 1983b). See Baumol and Willig (1985c, Appendix A) for support of the view that the rail industry is subject to extensive scale economies and must price well in excess of marginal costs.

78. See Baumol (1984a, 354–355). Baumol and Willig (1982, 30–31) state that intramodal rail competition forces rates to rail marginal cost:

> In the instances discussed . . . , it is interrail competition that most substantially affects the elasticity of demand for the railroad's services. The more intense the competition it faces, the more traffic a railroad will lose as a result of an increase in its rates. This is just another way of saying that increased competition increases the elasticity of demand for the affected services. It reduces the value of any given railroad's services to the customers because other options become available to them.
>
> Consequently, in competitive markets, demands will be relatively elastic and

> prices must be relatively closer to marginal costs. That is precisely why, in the case [of interrail competition], the price charged the shipper with alternative transport supply available must be relatively close to cost.

79. Baumol and Willig (1983a, 28).

80. Baumol and Willig (1983b, 36–37), Willig (1984a), and Baumol and Willig (1985a, 11).

81. Baumol (1982, 2, 5).

82. Transactions cost savings are widely recognized as a source of benefit for vertical mergers and restrictive vertical practices that are often disapproved by the antitrust laws. See Williamson (1979, 1985).

83. See, for example, Williamson (1974, 143) and Phillips (1975, 573).

84. Williamson (1979, 953–954, 960).

85. The paradox arises from the fact that efficiency gains from vertical integration and foreclosure may themselves depend on positive transactions costs and imperfect information. See Kaserman (1978).

4

Determination of Market Dominance and Maximum Reasonable Rates in the Transition to Deregulation

The basic of logic is the syllogism, consisting of a major and a minor premise and a conclusion; thus:

Major Premise: *Sixty men can do a piece of work sixty times as quickly as one man;*

Minor Premise: *One man can dig a post-hole in sixty seconds; therefore—*

Conclusion: *Sixty men can dig a post-hole in one second.*

Ambrose Bierce (1958, 79)

THE CONFLICT BETWEEN RAMSEY PRICING AND PERFECT CONTESTABILITY: THE MARKET MELTDOWN PROBLEM

Recent applications of the theory of contestable markets to practical problems of regulation and antitrust have produced surprising policy recommendations and revealed disturbing paradoxes. These applications told regulators that they should act as "a surrogate for competition unimpeded by entry barriers" and that the theory of contestable markets provides a welfare ideal that would serve as a vision of the competitive equilibrium to be sought in a transition to deregulation. However, faced with a belief that extremely discriminatory forms of Ramsey pricing cannot be achieved in highly contestable markets but are necessary to achieve firm viability, recent applications of the theory have elected to encourage movements away from contestability. Rather than serve as a promised benchmark for measuring departures from the welfare optimum, movements toward perfect contestability were believed to deprive incumbents of the sunk costs, cross-subsidies, and other barriers to entry and price competition believed needed for firm viability and sustainability. This chapter will demonstrate that a general belief that markets become unsustainable as one moves toward perfect contestability (a "market meltdown") seems to be driving the surprising welfare prescriptions advanced by applications of the theory.

This purported welfare dilemma will be illustrated by first showing that movements toward perfect contestability cause markets to become unsustainable in recent applications of the theory. Five proposed solutions to the unsustainability problem are considered, and it is shown that the only solution to the unsustainability problem consistent with the theory in a regime of increasing returns to scale is to impose departures from perfect contestability. The demonstration that none of these solutions to the unsustainability problem will work is somewhat tedious, but highly useful in illustrating why applications of contestability have been forced to advocate movements away from contestability to achieve sustainability. Additional problems of achieving sustainability are also found in the multimarket context. The results show that Ramsey pricing and perfect contestability are diametrically opposed concepts and this inconsistency is of more than theoretical interest. The puzzling policy prescriptions from recent applications of the theory are shown to arise from a belief that departures from contestability are needed for sustainability and achievement of Ramsey pricing efficiency gains.

HISTORICAL CONTEXT OF THE WELFARE DILEMMA

Whether the goals of promoting both revenue adequacy and intramodal rail competition are mutually exclusive is the oldest regulatory debate in the railroad industry. It actually originated in the historic dispute between Pigou and Taussig as to whether the very elaborate price discrimination observed in the rail industry reflected monopoly power or the necessity for demand-based joint-cost allocation (Locklin 1933; Ekelund and Hulett 1973).

Taussig argued that price discrimination in the rail industry was driven by what is now called "economies of scope," whereby different services were produced under conditions of joint costs. Revenue/marginal cost ratios among services would be greater than one and would differ by product line. Price discrimination would endure even under intense intramodal competition because it would be necessary for revenue adequacy.

Pigou argued that, on the contrary, rail rate discrimination arises from rail market power driven by economies of scale that permit price discrimination for essentially identical services among differently situated customers. Such discriminatory prices above marginal cost would be undermined by intramodal competition and could persist only under imperfect competition or monopoly.[1] Whether price discrimination reflected market power or the need to recover joint costs in the Pigou/Taussig dispute seemed to turn on whether the output in different markets was the "same thing."

New attempts to answer these old questions have been offered by applications of the theory of contestable markets to the problems of residual regulation in the rail industry by the Interstate Commerce Commission (ICC). Consistent with Taussig's position that prices in excess of marginal costs are not evidence of rail market dominance, applications of the theory (Baumol 1979; Willig 1984a) state that an industry configuration of contestable firms practicing Ramsey pricing is viable because such prices in excess of marginal costs are necessary for recovery of joint costs even when each of the firms produces the same multiple outputs and sells them in the same markets. Hence revenue/variable cost or revenue/marginal cost ratios are claimed to be misleading indicators of market dominance.[2]

The economic rationale for Taussig's model is most clearly articulated in the apotheosis offered to regulators when they are advised to employ contestability theory to act as a surrogate for competition. According to the argument, a multiproduct firm in "idealized competition," that is, a contestable market, enjoying economies of scope must satisfy only two requirements: (1) total revenues must equal total cost and (2) prices for each output must exceed marginal costs (yet be below Stand-Alone Cost [SAC]) as dictated by demand elasticities (which in turn are determined by the presence of competitors). In the apotheosis of a contestable market frequently cited, the lamb costs $10 to raise, $1 to shear, and $2 to butcher. The SAC of wool is $11 and mutton is $12. The example assumes that wool of one lamb sells for $7 and meat for $6, making it possible for a "full-line" competitor to recover all costs.[3] Citing this proverbial mutton/wool joint-cost allocation and pricing problem, it is concluded that revenue-adequate prices must exceed variable costs in order to recover joint costs and, therefore, prices exceeding marginal costs will be preserved even in a market with free entry (perfect contestability) and intense intramodal price competition among incumbents.

According to the theory, regulatory intervention in carrier pricing policies is unwarranted in such circumstances, and unrestrained competition among rail carriers would produce socially optimal Ramsey rate structures well above marginal costs (Baumol and Willig 1983b, 36–37). This vision of a deregulated rail industry is founded on a belief that such Ramsey prices could be achieved in an equilibrium of numerous multiproduct firms operating under multiproduct scale economies, setting prices above marginal costs in the same contestable markets without the benefit of a regulator. The theory of contestable markets would thus appear at first blush to offer new support for Taussig's position over that of Pigou in this historic dispute and to offer a conceptual rationale for the simultaneous achievement of deregulation, revenue adequacy, and vigorous intramodal competition in industries with firms enjoying multiproduct scale economies.

But Pigou's position also finds support from the theory of contestable markets. A fundamental theorem of contestability is that price (p) must equal marginal cost (mc) in a contestable market as long as the contested market is not a monopoly. In a contestable market occupied by multiple incumbents, the opportunity for profitable entry will erase discrepancies between price and marginal cost (Baumol, Panzar, and Willig 1982, 317; 1986, 344). The reason why price must equal marginal costs in a sustainable contestable market is highly instructive in resolving the Pigou/Taussig paradox. If an incumbent's price exceeds marginal cost, an entrant could profitably increase market share by producing a greater output (Δx) than an incumbent. The entrant need only offer to share with the incumbent's customers some part of the additional profit from the additional output, $(p - mc) \Delta x$, through an arbitrarily small price reduction. Given the assumptions of contestability, this cut will be sufficient to attract all of the contested incumbent's customers and Δx from another incumbent.

Contestability analysis ordinarily assumes the absence of price discrimination among customers (Baumol, Panzar, and Willig 1982, 333; Perry 1984). If this assumption is relaxed to allow either incumbent to attract rivals' customers with even transitory "special deals," price competition among incumbents can also be shown to force prices to marginal costs under contestability. The reason has profound implications for the sustainability of both multiple incumbents and a perfectly contestable monopolist pricing above marginal costs.

Assume two incumbent single-product firms in a contestable market with equal costs. Recall that contestability assumes an explicit lag in the price response of an incumbent to enable a new entrant to make a transitory profit with hit-and-run entry. If so, an incumbent as well as an entrant can exploit that pricing lag to profitably attract volume from another incumbent. Each firm can lure a customer from a rival in a contestable market by limiting the price reduction to that customer, and a discriminatorily low price (yet above marginal cost) will produce a transient profit opportunity during the hit-and-run period. Such incentives will motivate both firms, prices will be forced below average costs, and both firms will exit the industry.[4] The total vulnerability of a second firm to hit-and-run price cuts in a market made contestable by lags in the pricing response of incumbents means that the only sustainable equilibrium is a single firm. If the contestable market is composed of a sufficiently large number of firms (the above-cited case of perfect competition among shepherds), they will perceive that output can be profitably expanded even without a transitory price cut (demand is perceived by individual firms to be perfectly elastic). Furthermore, each incumbent will expand output until price equates to true marginal cost of each of the separate products of the multiproduct enterprise.

Indeed, applications of contestability theory implicitly also rely upon Pigou's position against Taussig when they reject the advice that regulators should promote contestability (ease of exit and entry) by "government intervention to insure equal access to the sunk facility" (Bailey and Baumol 1984, 124). One application (Baumol 1985a) endorses rail mergers between direct competitors on the grounds that intramodal competition drives prices to marginal costs, deprives carriers of the market power they need to engage in Ramsey pricing, and thereby produces revenue inadequacy, and that "it is appropriate to *do anything* which achieves adequate revenues as quickly as possible" (Baumol and Willig 1983b, 26, emphasis added). This public policy recommendation on rail mergers is based on nothing other than Pigou's position that prices above marginal costs needed for firm viability require imperfections in intramodal competition (departures from contestability).[5]

Despite the applications of the contestability theory to the contrary in railroad market dominance proceedings, direct price competition among incumbents who must price above marginal costs to be viable is not a sustainable industry equilibrium in highly contestable markets. This property of perfect contestability has profound implications when applied to existing industries undergoing a transition to deregulation, where firms are believed to need prices well above marginal costs for revenue adequacy. As will be shown below, contestability theory resolves the Pigou/Taussig dispute by showing that a movement towards perfect contestability will cause a "market meltdown" where a sustainable equilibrium of viable competing firms practicing Ramsey pricing is unattainable.

A market meltdown occurs when the ideal of perfect contestability is applied to existing industries with multiple firms believed to operate in regimes of economies of scale and scope. The perceived threat of unsustainability drives applications of contestability theory to impose either restrictions on price competition or restrictions on contestability (entry) to solve perceived unsustainability and nonviability problems. Five approaches to correct for this perceived problem of achieving an equilibrium have been implicitly or explicitly pursued in these applications: (1) demonstrate that sustainable and viable prices are actually equal to marginal costs (incumbents do not really demonstrate scale economies); (2) regulate prices and impose arbitrary "viability constraints" on the carriers; (3) invoke oligopoly theory to restrain price competition; (4) assume monopolistic competition among contestable firms operating with multiproduct scale economies in competitive markets; and (5) urge the suppression of intramodal price competition via mergers and vertical foreclosures so that prices will not be driven to marginal costs and carriers will have the market power necessary to engage in Ramsey pricing (i.e., conclude that the optimal industry structure is a contestable monopolist). Each of these will now be addressed.

PROPOSED SOLUTION NO. 1: ASSUME THAT PRICES DO IN FACT EQUAL MARGINAL COSTS

Recent applications cite contestability theory in ways that support both Pigou's position and that of Taussig. However, contestability theory can be used to show the extremely interesting result that, contrary to the beliefs of many economists, Pigou was right after all.

The fallacy that prices may exceed marginal costs of shepherds in a contestable market equilibrium of numerous firms was illustrated above: in a contestable market composed of many shepherds who perceive that output could be expanded at prices in excess of marginal costs, each would do so. Shepherds do not do so precisely because prices of mutton and wool do equal marginal costs. The theory of multiproduct scale economies developed in the theory of contestable markets illustrates this very interesting result.

Pigou's position that prices in excess of marginal costs are evidence of a market imperfection is widely accepted by economists for the case of single-product firms.[6] Taussig's model and its variant in contestability theory really amount to the argument that the multiproduct firm with economies of scope is a special exception. The claimed basis for the exception is that price must exceed marginal costs in the case of the multiproduct contestable market with more than one incumbent supplier because price must exceed marginal costs for each of the outputs by the amount necessary to recover the joint cost. This supposed exception for the multiproduct firm is widely accepted in the economic literature, which generally attempts to distinguish the single-product and multiproduct case.[7] But the single-product firm operating in the absence of scale economies does not need to price above marginal cost to recover fixed cost and neither does the multiproduct firm.

The distinction between product-specific economies of scale and economies of scope provides the fundamental insight necessary to resolve the dispute between the Taussig and Pigou models. Consider Panzar and Willig's "Fundamental Theorem of Multiproduct Scale Economies":[8]

$$S = \frac{w_1 S_2 + w_2 S_2}{(1 - S_c)} \tag{4–1}$$

where $C(q_1,q_2)$ = joint-cost function,

$$S_c = [C(q_1,0) + C(0,q_2) - C(q_1,q_2)]/C(q_1,q_2),$$

$$w_i = \frac{qi\ \partial\ C/\partial\ qi}{\Sigma\ q_j \partial C/\partial q_j}, \qquad i,j = 1,2$$

$$S_i = \frac{AIC_i}{\partial C/\partial q_i}$$

and

$$AIC_1 = \frac{C(q_1,q_2) - C(0,q_2)}{q_1}, \text{ for fixed } q_2 \text{ and similarly for } AIC_2. \qquad (4\text{–}2)$$

Equation 4–1 provides the degree of overall scale economies, S, meaning whether or not marginal cost pricing produces firm viability in the presence of well-defined cost functions. That index is the ratio of the weighted average of S_1 and S_2, the magnitude of "product-specific scale economies" for each output, where the weights are the revenue fractions if prices equal marginal costs, divided by one minus the degree of economies of scope (S_c). Economies of scope, in turn, are measured by the percentage of total cost saved by joint production rather than by the sum of Stand-Alone Costs (the cost of each product in isolation). Product-specific scale economies are defined to be the ratio of the average incremental cost (*AIC*) for the individual product line as defined in equation 4–2 divided by the marginal cost of that product line. Average incremental costs are the "avoidable costs" of each output divided by that output, holding output of the other product constant.

The Fundamental Theorem of Multiproduct Scale Economies definitively resolves the Pigou/Taussig dispute in a surprisingly simple way for the case of contestable markets. First we observe that prices must equal marginal costs if the market is occupied by many contestable firms. Even apart from Baumol's (1982) demonstration that prices above marginal costs would invoke profitable entry by a contestant, a contrary condition would produce an absurd result: one shepherd could profitably expand supply up to the entire industry output of mutton and wool by incurring additional incremental costs of feeding and grooming a single sheep as long as prices exceeded marginal costs.

If prices must equal marginal costs to prevent profitable entry and make the amount of mutton and wool produced by a single sheep determinate, what will determine whether prices equal to marginal costs will recover total costs (achieve firm viability)? The answer turns on the relationship between marginal costs and average incremental costs for the two outputs.

If $AIC_i = \partial C/\partial q_i$, there are no product-specific diseconomies of scale and there is no firm viability in a competitive equilibrium with numerous competitors charging marginal cost. However, weighted product-specific scale diseconomies may be sufficient to offset exactly the economies of scope, that is $\partial C/\partial q_i > AIC_i$, and there are no overall multiproduct scale economies. Marginal cost pricing will exactly recover total cost under these circumstances.

Figure 4–1 illustrates such results for the mutton and wool joint-cost production technology for the apotheosis discussed above. The terms in the figure are defined by equations 4–1 and 4–2. Average incremental costs are the extra costs of grooming and shearing an *individual sheep* ($1 for wool) and for feeding and slaughtering ($2 for mutton). The figure shows marginal costs must equal the respective prices ($7 for wool and $6 for mutton) but exceed average incremental costs (AIC) by just enough to recover the joint cost of the sheep itself to achieve firm viability.[9] Where the production technology is not well-behaved (kinked) at the equilibrium outputs, an analogous result can be derived by use of the procedure suggested by Kahn, whereby the supply schedule (and thus a measure of marginal costs) for each output is defined to be total incremental revenues of both joint outputs less the revenues from the complementary joint product.[10]

The skeptic who doubts that shepherds charge marginal costs and do not practice Ramsey pricing need only try the numbers in the hypothetical example in the formula. Assume that $7 for wool and $6 for mutton are marginal costs in Willig's hypothetical example. Assuming also that average incremental costs are $1 and $2, respectively, gives the known coefficient for multiproduct scale economies of 1.0 in equation 4–1. The correct result is that numerous shepherds can survive with marginal cost pricing and there are no multiproduct scale economies. But there is also no need for Ramsey pricing.

Ramsey prices exceeding marginal costs are just as unsustainable for the multiproduct firm facing direct competition from incumbents in a contestable market as they are for the single-product firm. Pigou, not Taussig, was right after all.[11] Market imperfections of some sort (such as departures from perfect contestability) are required to restrain price competition among incumbents and profitable entry when prices exceed marginal costs.[12]

Contrary to the "Taussig model" as endorsed in recent applications of contestability, whether price discrimination is necessary for firm viability does not turn on whether the two outputs are the "same thing" or not. The economics of the multiproduct case are identical to the single-product case and turn on whether $\partial C/\partial q_i > AIC_i$ by an amount just sufficient to permit marginal cost pricing to recover the joint costs.[13] If so, firms operate in a regime of constant returns to scale, and price discrimination is not

Figure 4–1
Shepherds Price Multiple Outputs at Marginal Cost (and Above-Average Incremental Costs)

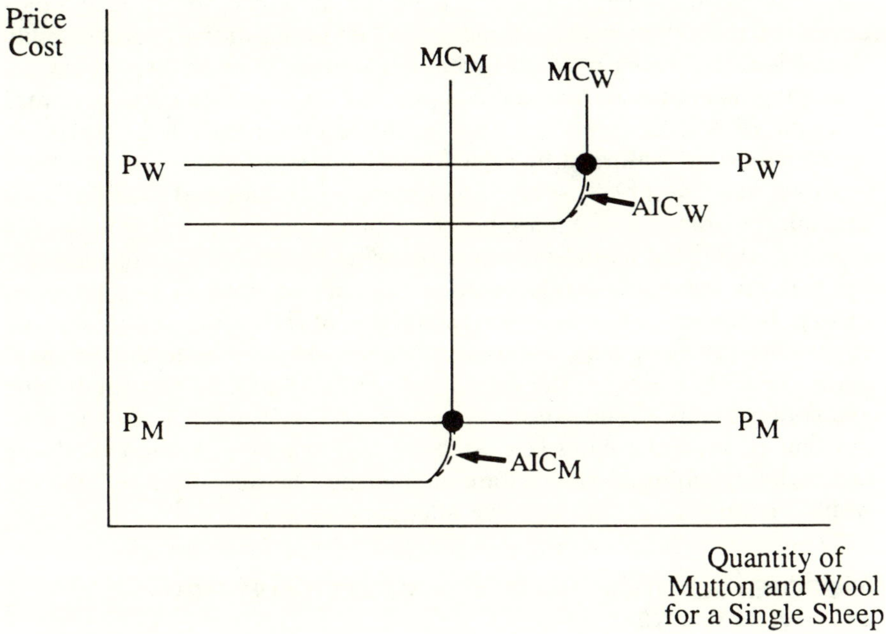

Legend:

P_M = Price of Mutton

P_W = Price of Wool

MC_M = Marginal Cost of Mutton

MC_W : Marginal Cost of Wool

AIC_M = Average Incremental Cost of Mutton

AIC_W = Average Incremental Cost of Wool

required for multiple incumbents to achieve viability while competing in the same contestable markets. If not, price discrimination above marginal costs is required for firm viability, but firms are not sustainable against entry in highly contestable markets occupied by more than one incumbent.

Most cost studies in the rail industry assume no product-specific scale economies or diseconomies (constant marginal and average incremental costs). Panzar and Willig's Fundamental Theorem of Multiproduct Monopoly (equation 4–1) implies that if this costing methodology is correct, the necessary conditions for multiproduct scale economy exist in railroading, and prices must exceed marginal costs. But in this case, shepherds, who must price at marginal cost in equilibrium, would not provide a paradigm for regulators in the rail industry. The implication of contestability theory is that seeking railroad revenue adequacy is inconsistent with encouraging maximum intramodal competition (and with movement toward a regime of perfect contestability of multiple incumbents as a "surrogate for competition" enforced by regulators).

Meyer and Tye (1988) suggest that scale economies and thus the need for Ramsey pricing above marginal costs have been exaggerated in the rail industry. If so, the model of shepherds would apply to the rail industry, but not for the reasons offered by recent applications of contestability theory. In this case, revenue adequate prices of rail carrier services would equal long-run marginal costs as they were shown above to do for shepherds. In such a regime, the purported conflict between Ramsey pricing and contestability would not exist, nor would the Pigou-Taussig paradox: movements toward greater contestability and price competition would be ordinarily unambiguously welfare enhancing, because Ramsey pricing would be unnecessary for revenue adequacy.

PROPOSED SOLUTION NO. 2: ASSUME ARBITRARY FIRM VIABILITY CONSTRAINTS

Braeutigam (1984) solves the sustainability problem for firms practicing Ramsey pricing while competing directly in the same contestable markets by assuming both arbitrary viability constraints for each firm and that an omniscient regulator establishes the necessary prices.[14] This approach achieves firm viability by constraining direct price competition among incumbents and by giving up the claim that the Ramsey prices are sustainable in an equilibrium of competing multiproduct contestable firms.

However, separate viability constraints for all firms in a contestable market operating in a regime of scale economies are a source of inefficiency that would be eliminated in a regime of contestability. (See Dewey 1958, for a demonstration in precontestability language.) In Braeutigam's model, multiple firms in the industry are assumed to be producing the same outputs with the same resources and operating under scale economies. Each threatens to contest all others' output should any firm set prices that exceed its total cost of production. If so, there is an economy of scope in producing all outputs that could be realized by a multiproduct entrant contesting output of all incumbents simultaneously. Since there are no barriers to entry, such a multiproduct entrant could eliminate all of the potential inefficiency arising from separate viability constraints, and by assumption, would be forced to produce the socially efficient outcome with zero profits.[15]

But there is another catch in the example: the relaxation of separate viability constraints eliminates "the pool of potential entrants" (Bailey and Baumol 1984) needed to ensure contestability along with the inefficient market structure.[16] Separate viability constraints with regulated prices serve to permit each competitor to contest the other's monopoly. After the multiproduct entrant successfully contests the market structure of the incumbent single-product monopolies, it becomes a multiproduct monopolist facing no threat of entry in this closed system.

Nor does Braeutigam's model purport to provide a "competitive market model" that justified a regime of permissive pricing rules by regulators in industries undergoing a transition to deregulation. Indeed, the model explicitly assumes Ramsey prices are established by regulators. Thus it does not appear to serve as (nor was it offered as) a model for regulators needed to justify the policy prescriptions of recent applications of the theory to leave pricing decisions up to a "weak invisible hand" (Baumol, Bailey, and Willig 1977).

Once again, these points may be illustrated by reference to the simple hypothetical example. Suppose we assume hypothetically that shepherds practice Ramsey pricing above marginal costs and that prices are constrained by regulators to achieve the arbitrary firm viability constraint. A new entrant could profitably expand the meat and wool of every sheep it raised by assumption, as compared with incumbents. Suppose the new entrant could produce the meat and wool of $N+1$ sheep by raising only N sheep. It would save the $10 necessary to raise that sheep plus all the incremental profits on the incremental wool and mutton of the N sheep. Since nothing would stop the entrant from successfully contesting the output of the entire industry, the market collapses to a monopoly. This development could be prevented in the model only if regulators fix prices and permit entry only to contest output of a single incumbent.

PROPOSED SOLUTION NO. 3: ASSUME OLIGOPOLY INTERACTIONS

The typical way economists solve the equilibrium problem in such circumstances (prices exceed marginal costs for multiple incumbents) is to assume that incumbents account for the pricing and output responses of a limited number of incumbents and entry is limited by barriers. For example, Levin (1981a, 1981b) assumes that railroads operate as oligopolists, and invokes "conjectural variations" to restrain output and price response even when price exceeds marginal cost. Such strategic behavior will break down in highly contestable markets, just as it does in oligopolies with sufficiently large numbers of firms.

Other models also assume departures from contestability to achieve an equilibrium. Beilock (1985) found empirical evidence supporting the existence of permanent price differentials in a highly competitive market. He speculated that the results were attributable to information cost differentials and difficulties of arbitrage. Borenstein (1985) shows that such permanent price discrimination can arise in oligopoly markets where firms produce differentiated products under returns to scale (but not economies of scope). Firms use sorting devices to identify customers with strong preferences for the differentiated product and price output to other customers closer to marginal cost. This discrimination is not undercut by the threat of entry because a new entrant would also have to recover the brand fixed cost. The model explicitly assumes the absence of economies of scope so that profitable simultaneous entry for multiple products cannot occur. Determinant results are achieved by assuming a particular oligopolistic reaction among incumbents.

Reverting to traditional oligopoly theory as the "competitive market model" for a deregulated rail industry with heavy sunk costs would leave little of the initial vision of contestability as an innovative welfare standard to guide regulators in the transition to deregulation. If a revenue adequate equilibrium is to be achieved by oligopolistic interactions of incumbents pricing above marginal costs, actions to enhance contestability could only detract from that objective by forcing incumbents' prices toward marginal cost to deter entry. Such advice to degrade contestability to achieve revenue adequacy would certainly represent a setback for the hope that the "unifying analytical structure" of contestability would replace oligopoly theory and "aspire to provide no less than a unifying theory for the analysis of industrial organization" to replace the theory of perfect markets (Baumol, Panzar, and Willig 1982, 320–321; Baumol 1982, 1–2, 15).

PROPOSED SOLUTION NO. 4: ASSUME A CHAMBERLAIN EQUILIBRIUM OF GEOGRAPHIC AND PRODUCT COMPETITION

The model of a firm both (1) Ramsey pricing well above marginal costs and (2) operating under multiproduct scale economies in a contestable market occupied by more than one firm producing identical outputs was shown above to be unsustainable. If competition between two such incumbents *in the same market* is unsustainable, perhaps an alternative would be competition among imperfect competitors, that is, monopolistic competition. Indeed, in most practical applications of contestability theory, members of the "pool of potential entrants" into individual contestable markets are also said to compete with incumbents via "geographic" or "product" competition as well as via the threat of entry.[17] These competitive alternatives are often not perfect substitutes in demand, but positive cross-elasticities are assumed as an additional constraint on the market power of incumbent firms operating in contestable markets.

Here it is useful to recall that economics already has an existing theory of a monopolist with no market power—the theories of monopolistic competition offered by Chamberlain (1933). If the theory of contestable markets has anything new to say, it should initially offer new insights when the predictions of the two models are compared (Baumol, Panzar, and Willig 1982, 382).

Chamberlain's model of monopolistic competition enforces a zero profit equilibrium with downward sloping average cost curves by assuming (a) entry to the "group" by suppliers of imperfect substitutes or (b) pricing/output responses of rivals offering imperfect substitutes. In the first case, short-run profit maximization induces entry by suppliers offering imperfect substitutes, shifts demand curves, and enforces a tangency of demand and average cost. In the second, shortsighted price cutting and mutually inconsistent and reinforcing output expansion force price to average cost in equilibrium.

In Figure 4–2, point *A* is the Chamberlain equilibrium, where *dd* is the demand curve derived by assuming that the group is sufficiently large that the monopolistic competitor does not perceive that producers of competing products follow the firm's price changes. The *DD* demand curve is derived by assuming that other competitors would match the individual monopolistic competitor's pricing decisions.

Contestability theory avoids the paraphernalia of monopolistic competition with its dependence on competition *among* differentiated product markets and its special assumptions about the output decisions of other suppliers in the "group." Like Chamberlain's demand curve, the demand curve of a contestable monopolist intersects a declining average cost curve at the market price, but by assuming that competition *for the market* forces suppliers to choose prices to deter entry. The "representative firm" and its two demand curves in Chamberlain's analysis are dispensed with under contestability, and the analysis is ceteris paribus. Thus it is of substantial interest to determine precisely what distinguishes the contestable equilibrium from the monopolistically competitive equilibrium.

Baumol, Panzar, and Willig (1982, 332; 1986, 358) note that Chamberlain's "high tangency" equilibrium in Figure 4–3 (point *B*) is not sustainable in a contestable market because a new entrant perceives that it can make a profit by charging a lower price. This, of course, should not be surprising, since *B* is not an equilibrium price in a monopolistically competitive market either. In the "large numbers" case, each firm will perceive a movement along the *dd* demand curve to be profitable. Chamberlain concluded that only if numbers were sufficiently small to eliminate the *dd* curve (i.e., produce an oligopoly) would the high tangency be an equilibrium.

Less obvious and not mentioned in Baumol, Panzar, and Willig (1982),

Figure 4–2
Chamberlain's Model of Equilibrium in Monopolistic Competition

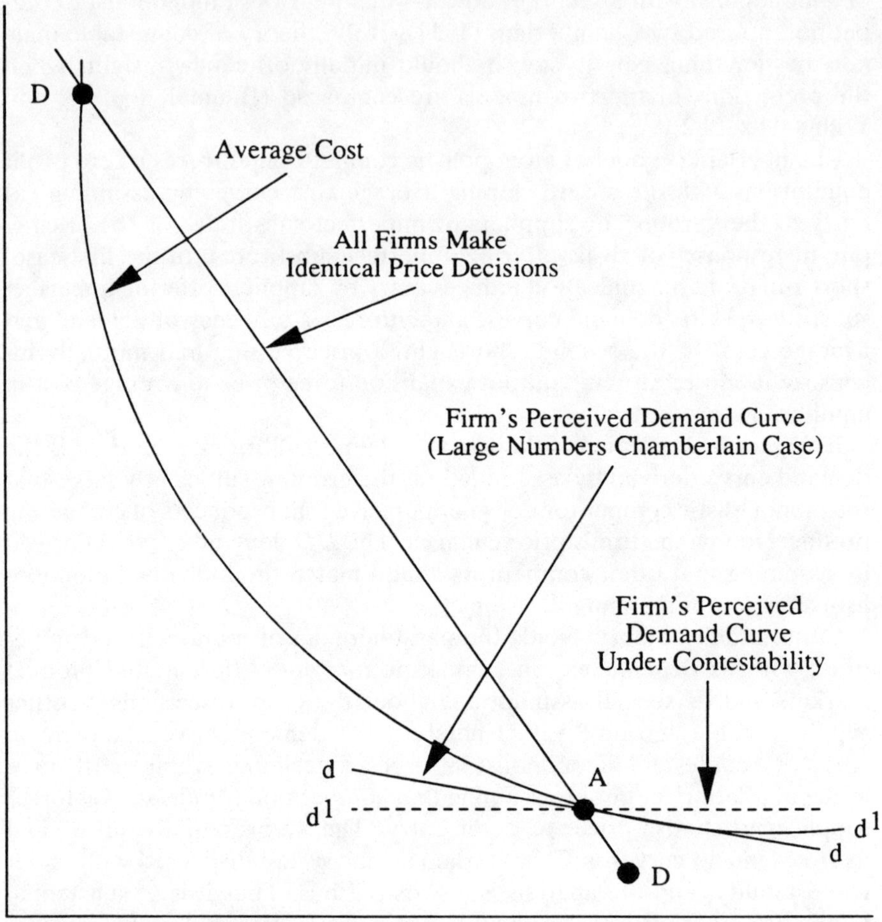

the "low tangency" Chamberlain equilibrium in Figure 4–2 is not sustainable in a contestable market either. The reason is that contestability's assumption of a lag in the price response of each of the monopolistic competitors makes a hit-and-run price cut profitable, just as it was shown to do above in the case of goods that were perfect substitutes.

In the usual contestability regime in which even temporary price discrimination is not allowed among purchasers of the same product (Baumol, Panzar, and Willig 1982, 333), Chamberlain's price competition among imperfect substitutes would appear to be redundant in light of the discipline of contestability. Any higher price would invoke entry and any lower price

Figure 4–3
Chamberlain's "High Tangency" Example of Monopolistic Competition

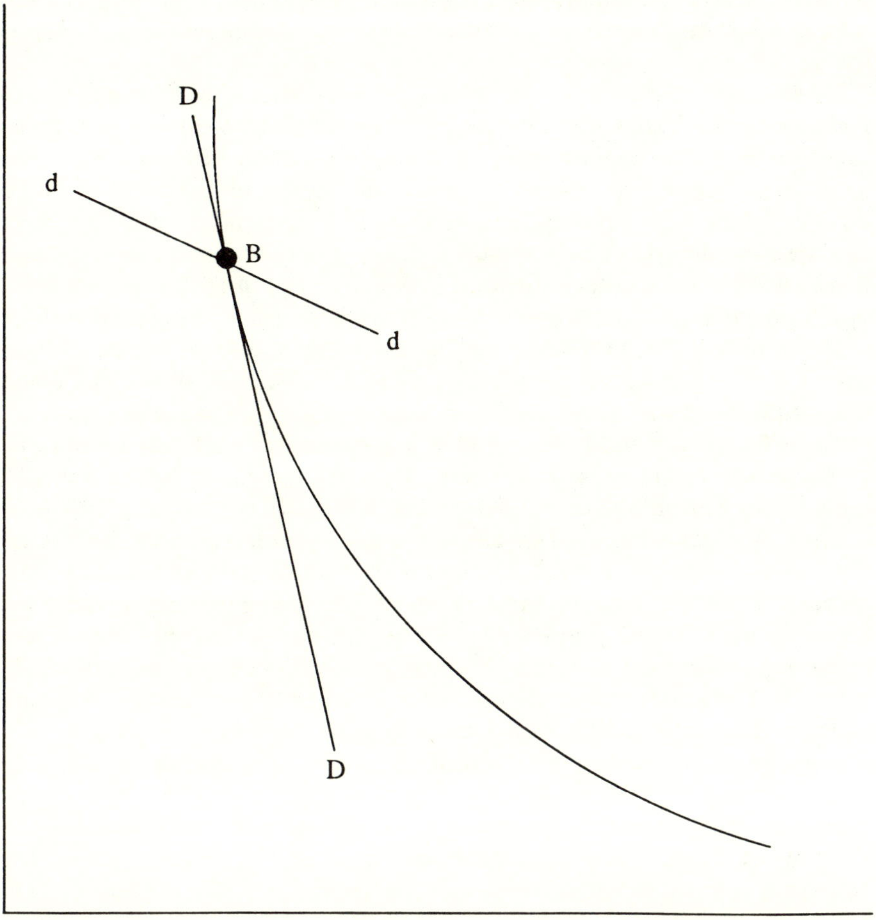

would force immediate exit by the incumbent. Assumptions regarding imperfect competitors' price responses would appear to be irrelevant to the firm's choice of price and output. Given the incumbent's lagged pricing responses, prices above average costs will always be deterred by hit-and-run entry before imperfect competitors respond with lagged price changes.

If the lagged price response of incumbent monopolistically competitive firms is redundant in light of instantaneous hit-and-run entry in a contestable market, the assumed instantaneous response of the customers of competing firms undermines sustainability once price discrimination (even temporary) is allowed in a monopolistically competitive contestable regime.

The reason is given above when it was shown that price must equal marginal cost in a contestable market composed of more than one firm producing perfect substitutes.[18] Intuition tells us that the fact that the profitable price decrease diverts customers from imperfect substitutes rather than perfect substitutes should be irrelevant to the unsustainability result, and such is indeed the case.

This is most easily shown for the single product case in Figure 4–2, but it can be readily extended to the multiproduct case. Contestability enforces the discipline of competition by assuming a price lag that forecloses the incumbent's ability to respond immediately to the entrant's lower price during the transitory hit-and-run period of exceptional profits. But if we assume a multimarket Chamberlain equilibrium of contestable monopolies, firms supplying imperfect substitutes will be restrained for an identical period in their ability to respond to the loss of volume arising from a price cut initiated by the supplier of an imperfect substitute. If so, entry by a price cutter will always appear to be profitable. The additional volume will always produce additional profits as long as price exceeds marginal cost, and this temporary additional profit will always allow a trivially small price decrease which will cause customers of the incumbent to switch immediately to the entrant.

Such profitable hit-and-run entry will occur under monopolistic competition for reasons identical to the reasons that force price equal to marginal cost for the case of multiple firms producing perfect substitutes. Suppose price exceeds marginal cost for a contestable monopolist engaging in monopolistic competition with other firms, all operating in contestable markets. The entrant approaches customers of an imperfect substitute and offers a contract to sell incremental output in the contested market at a temporarily lower price than the incumbent (P_1) (but one above marginal cost). Suppose an additional volume of Δq is contracted for by the new customers in response to the lower price. The entrant's additional profit per unit of the incumbent's production (q) is $(P_1 - mc) \Delta q \div q$. Any offer of a rate cut to the incumbent's current customers less than this will cause an immediate diversion of all of the incumbent's current customers during the hit-and-run period, but still leave a profit to the entrant from the sale of the extra output.

The key to successful entry is the ability to enforce a transient price discrimination scheme during the hit-and-run period between the incumbent's old customers and the newly attracted customers, made possible by the lag in price response by incumbents. Indeed, the contested incumbent and the suppliers of imperfect substitutes both become unprofitable if they were formerly in a tangency equilibrium, and they immediately exit the market during the hit-and-run period because they cannot respond in price as fast as they can exit.

The pricing lag of incumbents in contestability theory may be recast as the *dd* demand curve of monopolistic competition. As shown in Figure 4–2, Chamberlain's tangent *dd* curve will not be perceived to be the firm's demand curve during the period of hit-and-run entry. The dotted *d'd'* demand curve will be perceived during the hit-and-run period—producing exactly the same unstable result as the unsustainable high tangency in Figure 4–3 cited in Baumol, Panzar, and Willig (1982, 332).

Consequently, we have a profound result for the prospect that perfect contestability will replace perfect competition as the "standard of welfare-maximizing structure and behavior" (Baumol 1982, 2): contestability can be sustained only in the extreme case of a complete monopolist with zero demand elasticity,[19] and the more general case of a multimarket regime of contestable monopolistic competitors is unsustainable if contestability is enforced with pricing lags imposed on incumbents. Nothing new is added by the assumption that each firm is a multiproduct one, and the results are readily extended to the more general case of Braeutigam's (1984) regime of multiproduct firms producing imperfect substitutes.

What is profitable to an entrant is of course profitable to an incumbent, and the incumbent would already have been making discriminatory "special offers" to current patrons of imperfect substitutes. Although price discrimination is generally believed to contribute to firm viability in contestability theory, it produces unsustainability when contestable monopolistic competitors seek to employ it simultaneously.[20] Ramsey pricing above marginal costs necessary to achieve firm viability and movement toward perfect contestability once again are perceived to be fundamentally incompatible.

These results may be shown once again by returning to the hypothetical example of mutton and wool. Suppose prices of mutton and wool are $6 and $7, respectively. Suppose there are Ramsey prices and a shepherd incurs marginal costs of $2 and $1 for mutton and wool respectively, the same as the average incremental costs. Multiproduct scale economies and economies of scope therefore prevail. The shepherd is assumed to be a monopolistic competitor who competes against a rancher who sells beef and hides. Both face the threat of hit-and-run entry.

The successful entry strategy is quite simple. Suppose the shepherd is required by contestability theory to post prices for a period and leave them unchanged (see Chapter 3). The entry approaches current customers of the rancher and offers to sell mutton and wool for $5.90 and $6.90, respectively, during this period. Suppose prior customers of the rancher buy 100 units of mutton and wool each at the lower prices during this period. Assuming marginal costs are constant, the entrant earns $390 + $590 = $980. The contestable rancher cannot respond to this loss of volume because of the assumed lag in price response. The entrant shares $1 of the profit from entry with the shepherd's existing customers, who immediately abandon the incumbent because its prices are frozen during the hit-and-run period. The monopolistically competitive shepherd has no more defenses to prevent profitable entry than the atomistically competitive shepherd that attempts to charge Ramsey prices in a market occupied by more than one incumbent.

Contestablity analysis thus poses a "rock/scissors/paper" game for incumbents in monopolistically competitive markets. Contestability undermines the high tangency equilibrium in monopolistically competitive markets, but price competition in monopolistically competitive markets undermines a contestable low tangency equilibrium. Encouragement of contestability and price competition thus emerges as a villain producing unsustainability in practical applications of the theory.

Once the perfect contestability model is accepted as "no less than a unifying theory as a foundation for the analysis of industrial organization" (Baumol 1982, 15), the major problem facing regulators seeking a transition to deregulation is perceived to be the need to protect incumbents from unsustainability (failure to become revenue adequate). Proposals to promote contestability are viewed as frustrating the ability to achieve Ramsey pricing and firm viability. Roadblocks to price competition and entry such as denials of access by incumbents to their sunk facilities thus appear to be a step in the right direction and lead to the next proposed solution.

PROPOSED SOLUTION NO. 5: SUPPRESS INTRAMODAL COMPETITION

The surprising conclusions on competitive access issues in applications of contestability theory become understandable only in the context of the perceived unsustainability of monopolistic competition in contestable markets. The "overriding consideration" is argued to be achieving firm viability (Baumol and Willig 1983b, 29). Starting with this objective, the enhancement of contestability can only reduce degrees of pricing freedom believed needed by the regulated firm to achieve revenue adequacy (Phillips 1981). Indeed, if vigorous intramodal competition produces revenue inadequacy,[21] then the logical conclusion is that sunk costs, cross-subsidies, and so forth can improve welfare if they reduce price competition among incumbents. Promoting contestability via enhanced competitive access is thus rejected because it erodes the market power believed to be needed to practice Ramsey pricing in industries undergoing a transition to deregulation (Baumol and Willig 1985a, 1985b, 1985c; Tye 1987b; Meyer and Tye 1988).

The theory also has important implications for merger policy. Competition-reducing mergers are claimed to be in the public interest according to the theory precisely because they eliminate the competition among incumbents believed to drive prices to marginal cost, thus producing revenue inadequacy (Baumol 1985a).

Contestability theory has been cited to reject the possibility of anything other than cost-saving motivations arising from mergers of allegedly contestable monopolists. But the theory suggests that another plausible explanation for such mergers is also to eliminate the price competition among imperfect substitutes that is driving price below levels believed necessary for firm viability. The firm in a contestable market would find that such price competition would be quite costly to it and would be strongly attracted to merging with potential contestants for its markets. The quest to eliminate competition between incumbent contestable monopolists and potential entrants is what the theory would predict even without the presence of moderate economies of scope. Such mergers to degrade contestability would be particularly attractive if potential entrants were either few in number or if they needed to occupy a nearby geographic market in order to readily enter the geographic market in question. Rather than assuaging concerns over mergers, the existence of a high degree of contestability prior to the merger should raise new concerns over the merging companies' motives.

THE UNSUSTAINABILITY PROBLEM IN A MULTIMARKET CONTEXT

Contestable markets is too restrictive a term for what is in reality a set of complementary models. Single-market contestability analysis is nested within a broader structure of the theory of multiproduct market structure and an implicit theory of multimarket equilibrium. Additional problems of achieving multimarket sustainable equilibria are revealed in the context of this broader structure of theory and are sufficiently troublesome that they impose additional restrictions on the applicability of single-market contestability theory in the situations where it has been offered as an imprimatur for important policy decisions.

Contestability theory assumes that there is an infinite "pool of potential entrants" who are ready to engage in hit-and-run entry at no cost disadvantage, then exit the market and redeploy their resources. The analysis usually is a ceteris paribus consideration of a single market with no particular assumptions about the multimarket equilibrium in which these firms operate. The theory makes no particular assumptions regarding what the "pool of potential entrants" is doing for a living while it is awaiting the opportunity to contest a market (Cairns and Mahabir 1988). In practical applications, however, specific additional assumptions are being made about what these potential entrants are doing for a living. As the above discussion of contestable monopolistic competitors has shown, these assumptions can make the hypothesized contestable multimarket equilibrium unsustainable.

A regime of monopolists cannot threaten one another with hit-and-run entry while engaging in Chamberlain's imperfect price competition. As shown above, severe restrictions on *demand substitution* at the margin among entrants and incumbents (zero own and cross-elasticity) must sustain the equilibrium. Equally severe restrictions on *supply substitution* at the margin among entrants and incumbents can be shown also to be required.[22]

The conditions for a sustainable contestable monopoly pose a "paradox of supply substitution" in a multimarket context. For hit-and-run entry, members of the pool of potential entrants must have ready access to all the necessary resources to be an instantaneously effective alternative supplier. Supply substitution for the entire market must be "total," to use Shepherd's (1984) terminology. Potential entrants, too, must be operating in contestable markets while threatening entry. The ideal candidate would initially appear to be the incumbent in a nearby contestable market who could readily switch its capacity into the market in question. Such a candidate would appear to be ideal because it is presently supplying the same service using the same resources and technology but in a different geographic market, and could exit its current employment at no cost. In fact, most examples of contestability usually cite other airlines or water carriers that would simply switch routes in response to a hit-and-run profit opportunity (Baumol 1983a, 1984b, 1986; Bailey and Panzar 1981).

But, for the incumbent to be sustainable, it was shown above that it must also be impossible for the potential entrant to contest any arbitrarily small part of the incumbent monopolist's market while simultaneously retaining its own contestable monopoly. The absence of any entry barriers for the total output of the contestable market must paradoxically be combined with prohibitive entry barriers for what Shepherd (1984) calls "trivial entry."

The implicit restrictions on supply substitution among contestable monopolists and potential entrants are troubling because they may be either internally inconsistent or virtually impossible to meet in practice:

1. The contestable monopolist and potential entrant must use (or have instantaneous access to) common resources in their respective markets that are perfectly substitutable (the assumed absence of cost disadvantages to entrants).
2. The common resource is infinitely divisible over time in both the old and new employment (no sunk costs—the hit-and-run assumption).
3. At least one common resource must be used at less than minimum efficient scale (the monopoly assumption), and the common resource must be completely indivisible between the markets of the incumbent and potential entrant (it is "fixed" to one market only).

The difficulties of satisfying all these conditions simultaneously in a model of contestable monopolists serving alternative airline routes may be illustrated by a paradox suggested by Weitzman's theorem.[23] Suppose (to make the math simple) that actual demand per unit of time (T) in each route were $1/N$ of minimum efficient scale of the common resource whose underutilization was the source of the fixed cost. And suppose each carrier's cost function (C_i) was separable into identical factor inputs labelled "fixed" (F_i) and "variable" (C'_i) as a function of volume (V_i):

$$C_i = F_i + C'_i V_i, \text{ where } i = 1, \ldots, m. \qquad (4\text{–}3)$$

With perfect contestability, this proposed multimarket equilibrium is not sustainable because it can be contested profitably by a multimarket firm that simultaneously enters all such markets up to N. There is an "economy of scope" to the new entrant arising from the fact that the common resource whose cost is perceived to be fixed can be shared across routes by taking advantage of hit-and-run entry ("supply substitution" at the margin).

Since there are no entry or exit costs, the entrant produces at minimum efficient scale in the first market for a period of $1/N$ and sells from inventory for the remainder of that period in that market. The entrant proceeds to the next market and does the same, and so forth up to N markets. If the cost of inventorying supply after entry is too great, the entrant inventories demand prior to entering.[24] The savings in cost for the entrant is $(N-1)F_i$ per time period. Inventory costs can be driven toward zero by arbitrarily decreasing the cycle time (T) (Baumol, Panzar, and Willig 1983).

In the pure case, therefore, perfect hit-and-run opportunities will eliminate fixed costs among the pool of incumbents and potential entrants. Imperfect contestability could, however, be sufficient to achieve a sustainable equilibrium of both fixed andd sunk costs. Indeed, Baumol, Panzar, and Willig (1983, 491–492) offer purported counterexamples to Weitzman's claim of unsustainability of this sort in contestable markets by (1) assuming infinite inventory costs (e.g., instant perishability of airline service) and (2) assuming that "batch production" requires "an irreducible amount of production *time*." But infinite costs of inventorying supply often can be offset by inventorying demand (passengers simply wait for the next flight), and the assumption of a time restraint on exit only proves Weitzman's point. Fixed costs are achieved only by making them sunk, thereby eliminating the supposed distinction between fixed and sunk costs which is essential to contestability theory.[25]

In Baumol, Panzar, and Willig's (1983) airline route counterexample to Wietzman's point, a flight's duration is not infinitely divisible. All flights require the service of at least one pilot who cannot be costlessly moved from one route to another during a flight of finite time (pilot costs are sunk for some period) but whose services are used below minimum efficient scale on many flights (pilot costs are fixed up to a certain scale since manned aircraft requires at least one pilot regardless of size of plane).

More generally, the conditions to achieve a sustainable and viable multimarket equilibrium would be satisfied by strong indivisibilities in production technology between the services of the incumbent and the potential entrant's current line of business; that is, there must be extremely powerful entry barriers to simultaneously "sharing the indivisibility" (i.e., the source of each scale economy) between the potential entrant's market and the incumbent's market. The indivisibilities necessary for monopoly must confer strong "product-specific returns to scale" in the monopolist's and the potential entrant's market without also conferring economies of scope to the joint production of both products or services simultaneously.[26] As Baumol, Panzar, and Willig's (1983) counterexamples illustrate, this is likely to be accomplished by sunk costs. Once again, a departure from perfect contestability appears necessary to achieve firm viability and sustainability against the threat of profitable entry.

APPLICATION TO THE AIRLINE EXPERIENCE

The less than satisfactory experience with the predictions of the theory to the airline industry could perhaps be explained in part by the failure to consider the necessary restrictions on the multimarket relationships between the incumbent and potential entrant discussed above. Indeed, applications of contestability theory to airline markets specify multimarket conditions that explicitly violate the necessary sustainability conditions.

For example, Bailey and Panzar (1981) assert that a particular airline route is a contestable market and offer as candidates for the potential entrant carriers serving other routes. In practice, such potential entrants are argued to engage in hit-and-run entry readily because they are presently employing similar resources to supply similar services in a nearby alternative geographic market.

If each can engage in marginal supply substitution by shifting the common resource whose indivisibility is the source of scale economies in the two markets, the scale economies would be eroded and the two markets would collapse to a single multiproduct monopoly. Indeed, merger applicants inevitably perceive that a merger between two contestable monopolists will be profitable precisely because it offers the opportunity of breaking down frictions on supply substitution of underutilized resources.

The separate firms supplying the total output on each of the routes are simultaneously also being offered as mutual sources of strong geographic or source competition to one another. If they are considered to be even imperfect substitutes by travelers, price cannot exceed marginal cost in equilibrium as shown above. The markets for the incumbent and potential entrants then collapse to a single monopoly over all affected routes.

The difficulties of achieving sustainability in a regime of highly contestable monopolistic competitors may well help explain certain recent developments in the airline industry. Periodic rate wars drive rates below levels believed necessary for firm viability, while a "merger mania" continues unabated, despite studies that conclude that there are no efficiency gains from size. (See, for example, Caves, Christensen, and Tretheway 1984.) The potential anticompetitive threat from such mergers is dismissed because of the assumed protections of contestability. But anticompetitive airline mergers would appear attractive according to the logic of contestability theory precisely because they eliminate destabilizing price competition, achieve economies of scope by breaking down the indivisibilities that create scale economies, and reduce the size of the "pool of potential entrants."

CONCLUSION

The perception of major sustainability problems in markets approaching perfect contestability thus explains the surprising fact that applications of the theory often conclude that departures away from contestability are, in practice, welfare enhancing. These policy recommendations represent a significant reversal of the prior conclusion that the theory supported the elimination of frictions on contestability in industries undergoing a transition to deregulation. These perceived sustainability problems also pose questions as to how contestability analysis can achieve its objective of replacing perfectly competitive markets as the standard of welfare-maximizing structure and behavior. A somewhat unexpected result of this examination is the identification of limiting necessary conditions to achieve sustainability and viability of contestable markets in the hypothesized multimarket equilibria in which the theory has been applied.

The lessons from these applications of the theory also offer constructive suggestions as to how the theory of contestable markets can take its rightful place as an analytic tool and as a guide to economic policy. The theory as yet provides no clear guidelines for correct policy decisions in situations of imperfect contestability. Movements toward perfect contestability may be viewed in practice as creating static welfare losses by restricting the set of prices available as candidates for Ramsey pricing, or even by preventing a sustainability equilibrium entirely (a failure to achieve firm viability in a "market meltdown"). But movements toward perfect contestability promise to achieve the *x*-efficiency objectives of no excess costs or profits and the prospect of dynamic efficiency gains from a successful transition to deregulation. Movements toward perfect contestability have thus been viewed ambiguously in applications of the theory. Appropriate policy judgments therefore require a trade-off of the opposing welfare effects of any proposed change in market structure when one applies the theory to regulatory and antitrust problems in industries undergoing a transition to deregulation.

NOTES

1. The conflicts in the Pigou/Taussig debate have their analogue in the historical swings of national transportation policy between emphasis on competition and emphasis on revenue adequacy in the rail industry. Most recently, the Staggers Rail Act has called for achievement of both in a transition to deregulation. The perception that these regulatory goals are in conflict is the most significant regulatory policy issue facing the rail industry today, and unspoken answers seem to motivate the positions of the various interested parties on a wide variety of issues such as rail merger policy. For example, the U.S. Court of Appeals for the District of Columbia (1984), in rejecting the ICC's decision to grant a total exemption from regulation for rail transportation of export coal, which had been justified on the grounds that unregulated railroads would engage in efficient Ramsey pricing, stated that:

> The regime of price discrimination envisioned by the Commission clearly assumes some significant degree of railroad monopoly power. . . . It is well established that the ability of a firm to price discriminate is an indicator of significant monopoly power.
>
> . . . The Commission's opinion predicts a pricing regime in which there will not be an absence of market power with respect to shippers. Indeed, the regime is premised on the railroads' use of market power.

2. See Willig (1984a):

> *The degree to which price exceeds marginal cost does not indicate anything about the presence or absence of effective competition* [emphasis added] unless price exceeds stand-alone cost. The price will be set on the basis of demand. . . . Thus, where there are common costs, the division of those costs among the items produced does not necessarily indicate anything about the degree of competition facing the railroad. This is because, *even in a market with idealized competition* [emphasis added], the competitors will price each type of item according to its value to customers, up to the point at which the total revenue from all of the items sold equals the total cost of producing them. Values to customers may differ even if the railroad faces intense competition, and prices for transportation may differ as costs for competitors differ [footnote omitted].

Likewise, Baumol (1983c) stated that airline reservations systems were not natural monopolies (17), but also that prices should deviate from marginal costs in a competitive market (27–30) and that such results are consistent with Ramsey pricing and economic efficiency (37–38).

3. Willig (1984a, 15–16).

4. Note that the absence of barriers to exit implies immediate exit of unprofitable firms serving contestable markets.

5. See Baumol and Willig (1982, 30–31) for statements of concern that intramodal rail competition will drive price to marginal cost and violate the firm viability requirement.

6. The "Lerner Index," or (price − marginal cost)/price, has long been offered as a measure of market power, or at least imperfect competition. See Lerner (1943),

Landes and Posner (1981), Schmalensee (1979, 1982), and the discussion in Chapter 1.

7. In the literature, price discrimination is often believed to be necessary for revenue adequacy for multiproduct firms in perfect competition among one another, but evidence of market imperfections if the outputs of the two firms are the "same thing." See, for example, Ekelund and Hulett (1973); Kahn (1970, 94); Bonbright (1961, 355–356, 380–381); and Frank (1983).

8. Panzar and Willig (1977a) and Willig (1979b).

9. In the case of mutton and wool, where costs are well-behaved, shepherds will incur marginal costs of additional feed up to the point where they equate to revenues from additional mutton and likewise for grooming and other marginal costs of increasing the output of wool. Since these marginal costs will rise steeply at the equilibrium output, prices will equal marginal costs but be sufficiently above average incremental costs to recover the joint cost (defined as total cost less the sum of each of the avoidable costs) if shepherds achieve firm viability.

10. Alfred Kahn shows that, in the absence of well-defined marginal costs at the equilibrium outputs, the classic mutton and wool joint-cost pricing problem can be resolved by reference to demand prices for each (set by competition with other products). Kahn indicates that revenues from the second commodity may be netted out of the total revenue requirement to determine the required revenues from the first commodity, a measure of marginal cost defined by the effective supply function. See Kahn (1970, 1:77–83, 1:93–94 n.11). Note that Kahn's approach assumes that sheep, mutton, and wool come in fixed proportions and does not address the more general case in equations 4–1 and 4–2 where the proportions can be changed at an incremental cost. Note also that Kahn's definition of marginal cost differs from that of Figure 4–1, which assumes that the number of sheep and output of the other complementary product is held constant (which is another way of saying that Figure 4–1 does not assume fixed proportions).

11. Baumol (1982) suggests a variant of the above approach, but it applies to the single-product firm. Here costs of multiple incumbents are assumed constant over the relevant range. Or course such firms are pricing at marginal and average cost and there is no need for Ramsey pricing to become revenue adequate. This, of course, does not solve the sustainability problem where the firms operate under scale economies.

12. Note that this is a limited statement that prices in excess of marginal cost indicate departures from perfect competition, not that they are indicia of monopoly power.

13. This is exactly the same situation as for the single-product firm where price equals marginal cost but exceeds average variable cost by exactly the average fixed costs.

14. See also Braeutigam (1985). Braeutigam (1979) does not purport to solve the problem because the model assumes that the regulated mode competes against firms with constant returns and concludes that second-best Ramsey prices may be unachievable in practice.

15. Baumol, Panzar and Willig (1982, 312, 314, 333–334, 337–340) observe that "a viable firm Ramsey optimum will generally not be sustainable" in contestable markets.

16. See Spence (1983, 988) for discussion of an unsustainable "Viable Firm Ramsey Optimum."

17. See Tye (1984d) for description of product and geographic competition.

18. Spence (1983, 988) notes that demand plays little role in contestability analysis to date.

19. Baumol (1982, 5) states that the profit opportunity from price in excess of marginal cost "crumbles into dust" as long as the contestable volume is "fixed." The average revenue curve implicitly assumes no possibility of transitory price discrimination by the new entrant and no elasticity of demand (no competition from even imperfect substitutes).

20. Hidden assumptions about sunk costs thus are implicit in all sorts of equilibrium in economic theory. For example, Baumol, Panzar, and Willig (1982, 332) point out that quantity Cournot oligopolists are not sustainable under perfect contestability.

21. Baumol and Willig (1985c) provide numerous examples where prices are driven down to marginal costs by intramodal competition.

22. In most situations involving allegations of monopoly, the usual answer by the defendant is in the form of competition at the margin from both supply and demand substitution. Strong competition of this sort is proscribed by the theory of contestable monopoly markets for the incumbent and potential entrant, as the theory of contestable markets precludes them from being part of the same relevant market in any way that would prevent prices greater than marginal costs. For a discussion of concepts of defining the relevant market for antitrust, see Fisher (1979).

23. Weitzman (1983, 486–487) notes "a hit and run technology makes the firm behave 'as if' it is competitive in a market precisely because the convexity preconditions for competition are de facto being met in that market." Likewise, Shepherd (1984, 576) asserts a contradiction between "total entry" and "trivial entry."

24. The entrant would use the proposal (Baumol, Panzar, and Willig 1983) to sign contracts prior to entering, which is a device to inventory demand as well as reduce postentry risk of price retaliation.

25. Invoking indivisibilities of time that require the entrant to achieve a minimum efficient scale of production for inventory or to stay in the market for some minimum period explicitly violates the requirement that in a contestable market "any firm can leave without impediment, and in the process of departure can recoup any costs incurred in the entry process. . . . Even a very transient profit opportunity need not be neglected by a potential entrant. . . . Any positive profit means that a transient entrant can set up business." See Baumol (1982, 4).

26. Willig (1980, 143). Panzar and Willig (1977, 16) note that their examples of nonsustainability employ the assumption of weak economies of scope, strong demand substitution between products, and strong product-specific scale economies.

5

Conclusions on Recent Applications of Contestability Theory

The initial vision of the theory of contestable markets was to provide "a standard of welfare-maximizing structure and behavior." The "unifying analytical structure" of contestability theory "aspire[s] to no less than a unifying theory for the analysis of industrial organization." In applications of the theory, regulators were told that firms facing the threat of contestability would voluntarily adopt Ramsey optimal price structures and regulators should act as a "surrogate for competition unimpeded by entry barriers."

In many applications of the theory, however, perfectly contestable markets did not serve as the promised benchmark for measuring departures from the welfare optimum. Indeed, movements away from contestability were labeled as welfare enhancing. Movements toward greater contestability purportedly reduced the feasible set of Ramsey prices and thus welfare, either by enhancing buyer defenses to evade the income transfer schemes inherent in the price discrimination or by creating incentives for profitable entry at prices above marginal costs. Movements toward perfect contestability were believed to deprive incumbents of the sunk costs, cross-subsidies, and other barriers to entry and price competition believed needed for firm viability and sustainability and to give full latitude to welfare-enhancing price discrimination. Conversely, restraints on contestability were justified as expanding the price set available for the Ramsey pricing monopolist to achieve static efficiency gains.

The belief that contestable markets are inherently unsustainable and firms become nonviable as one removes impediments to perfect contestability thus seems to be driving the surprising welfare prescriptions advanced by applications of the theory. But the conclusion that contestability must be degraded in practice to achieve welfare gains is troubling for the widespread belief that perfect contestability defines the welfare optimum and that Ramsey pricing is achievable by a contestable monopolist. (See, for example, Morrison and Winston, 1987.) This conclusion is particularly worrisome in the light of findings of Schwartz and Reynolds (1983), Schwartz (1986), and Stiglitz (1987) that small departures from perfect contestability can produce major differences in market performance.

IMPLICATIONS FOR PUBLIC POLICY

The theoretical puzzles raised by applications of the theory of contestable markets translate directly into important policy choices in industries undergoing a transition to deregulation. Without clearly articulating the issues, application of the contestability theory to industries undergoing a transition to deregulation implicitly forces a policy choice between the goal of revenue adequacy and the goal of promoting competition. The suggested choice implicit in the endorsement of Ramsey pricing and the SAC test for the rail industry is to grant little protection to captive shippers in the transition and to encourage a posttransition industry structure characterized by substantially reduced intramodal competition.

The supposed need for extreme forms of price discrimination thus becomes the imprimatur for a variety of anticompetitive policy recommendations (Meyer and Tye 1988). These policy recommendations further encourage the search by the incumbent for the means to restrict competition and enforce Ramsey pricing, which is the only means offered to achieve revenue adequacy. The danger is that the theory will frustrate the transition to deregulation by fostering the impression among the regulators that revenue adequacy is incompatible with procompetitive goals. There clearly is no role for deregulation and competitive entry to achieve economic efficiency if all the problems of the industry have already been solved by Ramsey pricing. Indeed, competition will only make matters worse by eliminating opportunities otherwise available to the revenue-seeking price discriminator. This leads almost inexorably to a justification for whatever additional contrivances are necessary to protect the revenue interests of incumbents against the threats of competition. Since a "fair rate" is for all practical purposes whatever emerges from the extant restraints on competition that persist during the transition, it is only one more step to endorse whatever additional restrictions are necessary to achieve the goal of revenue adequacy above all else.

The ultimate creation of this train of logic is a revenue-adequate rail monopolist engaging in Ramsey pricing. Unless one is prepared to assume that the rail industry competes in contestable markets, the result is a pessimistic appraisal of the long-run prospects for reconciling the Staggers Rail Act goals of revenue adequacy, intramodal competition, and a transition to deregulation. Public policy thus seems to be slipping back into a dangerous pessimism over the viability of intramodal competition in the rail industry—a pessimism that has long plagued the history of transportation policy. If allowed to continue long, this pessimism can only result in regulatory decisions that lead to a substantial reduction in the very competition that was the initial rationale for deregulation.

AN ALTERNATIVE TO THE CONTESTABILITY VISION IN THE TRANSITION TO DEREGULATION

But what is the alternative? Meyer and Tye (1988) propose a "contractual equilibrium" in which firms use contracts to protect themselves from opportunistic behavior during the transition to deregulation. Contrary to the prescriptions of the proponents of contestability theory, this framework treats pricing efficiency and other static welfare gains as secondary to promoting a successful transition to deregulation. Procompetitive policies to enhance contestability are thus ordinarily treated as unambiguously desirable in this framework. The contractual equilibrium may be thought of as an extension of Coase (1960) in that regulators are invited to conduct "thought experiments" to determine what regulatory surrogates for contracts are necessary during the transition.[1] The ultimate objective is to replace transitory regulation with the contracts that would have been in effect had they not been superseded by regulatory institutions. The revenue/variable cost test discussed in Chapter 3 may be thought of as an example of a regulatory rule motivated by the contractual equilibrium concept.

The contractual equilibrium approach is also illustrated by a proposed methodology for pricing trackage rights offered by Tye (1988) when the ICC seeks to preserve the competition that would otherwise be eliminated by a rail merger. According to the contractual approach, the place to begin in establishing appropriate regulatory rules for pricing trackage rights is by constructing a thought experiment on how competition works to preserve competitive access in unregulated industries where the necessary divisions of revenues are subject to contracts.

Prior to the Staggers Rail Act, regulation previously served the courts' function of enforcing and regulating contracts in unregulated markets by preventing opportunistic behavior among rail carriers serving joint-line traffic. These privately negotiated but regulatory-enforced revenue division agreements typically force all owners of track to share positive and negative revenue variances proportionate to costs (since they are presumed to be the fault of neither carrier and such a division structure motivates the carriers to act jointly to eliminate revenue deficiencies). Meanwhile, each bears (enjoys) entirely any negative (positive) cost variances, which, for the most part, are under each carrier's control on the joint movement. Such revenue division agreements accomplish a rough standard of competition on equal terms and have until recently been the norm in the rail industry. Until the Interstate Commerce Commission took a permissive view toward their unilateral cancellation, these agreements had been changed primarily by the intervention of regulators. Although traditionally enforced by regulation and not the courts, such agreements are clearly consistent with the types of contractual understandings that would have been negotiated by carriers in unregulated markets prior to incurring sunk costs. Such revenue division agreements or their surrogates provide a useful starting point for defining competition on equal terms.

One might object that this proposed contractual equilibrium of competition on equal terms might be only one of the possible sets of contractual means to assign risks of revenue variances signed by the carriers prior to sinking costs. Further thought experiments would suggest a variety of plausible, previously agreed-upon schemes for allocating risk of revenue and cost variances. "Throughput agreements" and "take-or-pay" contracts are often signed in the transportation industries precisely to shift risk of revenue variances away from the suppliers who have sunk costs in the right-of-way to the suppliers of the operating services or shippers who are presumably more knowledgeable about their future demands or who are better able to bear the risks.

Alternative ex ante "visions" of a competitive contracting process in the absence of sunk costs as standards for achieving competition on equal terms for trackage rights thus cannot be rejected outright. In fact, they are considered in detail in Tye (1988). However, the chief alternative to competition on equal terms being offered to the rail industry is the parity principle under voluntary negotiations, that is, a price squeeze by the bottleneck carrier, conducted retroactively after the carriers have sunk their costs. It has little credibility as a prior vision of a contractual equilibrium since it assumes the connecting carrier naively grants the bottleneck carrier the ability to impose the scheme unilaterally and retroactively after costs have been sunk.

As a practical matter, the ICC may choose among proposals for pricing trackage rights rather than imposing a rigid formula. The choice should seek to accomplish the following procompetitive goals for trackage rights (Tye 1988):

1. Preserve premerger competition in the relevant markets to ensure the longer-run transition to competition as a substitute for regulation;

2. Encourage incentive compatibility in costing on the part of all carriers by making them bear (enjoy) their negative (positive) cost variances;
3. Allocate systemwide negative and positive revenue variances between tenant and landlord on equal terms;
4. Prevent cross-subsidy among potentially competitive and bottleneck services;
5. Encourage mergers designed to achieve true efficiency gains and discourage mergers designed to capture quasi-rents by foreclosing competitive access; and
6. Seek to achieve incentive compatibility in pricing decisions to the maximum extent consistent with the above objectives; the tenant should be discouraged from pricing decisions for the total service that impose an artificial and avoidable handicap on the landlord's ability to remain or become revenue adequate in providing track space.

A trackage rights price designed to encourage competition on equal terms may be thought of as a means of allowing regulators to approve intramodal rail mergers to achieve efficiency gains that would otherwise also result in anticompetitive route closures motivated by (quasi-) rent-seeking behavior. These incentives are thwarted by imposing, as a condition for the merger, contractual protection against opportunistic behavior that would have been precluded by contracts signed prior to sinking costs in the absence of regulation. What the policy merely states is that regulators will not put the imprimatur of antitrust immunity on mergers that can potentially create incentives for anticompetitive behavior via new opportunities for vertical foreclosures of competition. Competition on equal terms thus emerges as an admonition to preserve postmerger rail competition rather than as a rigid formula.

OVERVIEW: CONTRIBUTIONS OF CONTESTABILITY TO THE POLICY DEBATE

Prior to the advent of contestability theory, economists tended to dismiss sunk costs as "bygones" and thus irrelevant. The theory teaches us that this is not true. Elimination of sunk costs can be highly destabilizing to achievement of a competitive equilibrium. Indeed, the application of contestability theory to practical problems of deregulation may have shown that it is well-nigh impossible to achieve a competitive equilibrium in many theoretical situations. An overarching achievement of contestability theory has been to demonstrate that sunk costs underlie most equilibria in economics in ways that were previously poorly understood.

Recall that the initial objective of the theory was to provide a model of market structures that encompassed the entire spectrum of cost structures.

Market imperfections were defined, not in terms of departures from marginal cost pricing, but in terms of barriers to hit-and-run entry.

However, we have seen that pricing above marginal costs requires departures from perfect contestability, just as it requires a market imperfection in the conventional theory it sought to replace. The apparent impossibility to achieving a sustainable and viable equilibrium of firms practicing Ramsey pricing has so far dashed the hope that perfect contestability will serve as a paradigm which encompasses all cost structures. Skeptics who all along agreed with Pigou that pricing above marginal costs represents a market imperfection will of course really not be surprised that such pricing withers in the face of the most extreme form of perfect competition—costless and riskless hit-and-run entry.

The evolution of applications of contestability theory may be thought of as a series of efforts to protect an incumbent's need to be viable via Ramsey pricing from the perceived threat of profitable entry caused by pricing above marginal costs. The principal difficulty is to achieve the proper balance of threat and defense. Note that the discipline of contestability requires that entrants threaten incumbents with sufficient credibility to eliminate excess profits. But if incumbents always have the same postentry competitive advantages as entrants, they could via the same logic immediately deny entrants the postentry excess profits that are necessary to elicit entry. The assumption of a pricing lag for incumbents is a somewhat arbitrary attempt to impose the necessary asymmetry between incumbent and entrant in the postentry world. But we have seen that this handicap is too strong when the incumbent prices above marginal cost because contestable suppliers of either perfect or imperfect substitutes can use it to divert business from the incumbent at a profit during the hit-and-run period.

We can go one step further and state another problem: the pricing lag is not a sufficient condition to permit postentry profits by the entrant during the hit-and-run period. The focus on the contest between the entrant and incumbent has ignored entirely the existence of the rest of the "pool of potential entrants." No such handicap of a pricing lag has been imposed on them. They are still free to contest the entrant's excess profits and can eliminate those excess profits with the same competitive advantages that led to the conclusion that the incumbent must deter entry by pricing at competitive levels. If the threat of hit-and-run entry is to be presumed, all remaining members of the pool of potential entrants must also be handicapped with the pricing lag in the postentry competitive world—an arbitrary restriction indeed.

These difficulties all arise from the fact that the model is, as yet, ceteris paribus and the theory does not consider the problem in a multimarket framework. Until the contestability model is expanded to a multimarket general equilibrium and the sustainability problem is explicitly addressed, applications of the theory for firms practicing Ramsey pricing will be plagued with the perception of a market meltdown at perfect contestability.

While this means that contestability theory has so far failed in its efforts to supplant the entire spectrum of conventional theory with the notion of a contestable monopolist, it does not necessarily imply that the exercise has not borne fruit. Chapter 4 showed, for example, that contestability theory has provided new insights into the oldest issues in railroad rate regulation. It has provided a basis for definitively solving the Pigou/Taussig paradox—no small feat.

Applications of contestability theory have permitted equally significant understandings of many of the paradoxes raised by the economic theory of vertical foreclosures. The significance of these contributions may best be understood by reference to the ambiguous role of the Coase theorem in the Chicago School permissive model of vertical foreclosures. According to the Coase theorem, the efficiency rationale for government intervention into economic disputes ultimately arises from the presence of transactions costs. The genius of Coase (1960) was to point out that it did not matter what a judge decided if there were no transactions costs obstacle to recontracting. If the resulting outcome of a judicial or regulatory decision was inefficient, then the parties would voluntarily recontract to eliminate the inefficiency. (In the law, it is called an out-of-court settlement.)

The gist of Coase's vision was that the judicial and regulatory endowment of property rights could affect the achievement of the efficient outcome. Only if any inefficient decision can be costlessly reversed through contracts is there indifference to the distribution of wealth (property rights). But pursuit of efficiency gains rather than distribution of income nevertheless was at least implicitly assumed to be the proper standard for jurists and regulators.

The presence of transactions costs would appear to play a major role in any judicial intervention into private disputes and thus in the relative weights which should be assigned to equity and efficiency in making the correct judicial decisions. But things are not as simple as they seem.

Another progeny of the Chicago School was the development of an elaborate set of justifications for a permissive approach to a wide variety of "single firm" acts in vertical economic relationships—that is, policies established by a single firm which putatively possessed market power which allowed it to affect competition in upstream (supplier) and downstream (buyer) markets. These relationships had previously been treated highly skeptically in the antitrust law on vertical restraints: resale price maintenance, dual distribution, exclusive dealing, territorial restrictions, and so forth. Relevant legal concepts which constrained these unilateral actions involved merger policy, tying, monopoly leveraging, essential facility, bottleneck, price squeeze, and vertical foreclosure.

However, the Chicago School urged a permissive approach to vertical foreclosures on the grounds that the availability of a "perfect price squeeze" would create incentives for monopolists actually to encourage competition at prior or subsequent stages in a vertical market relationship so that the efficiency advantages of entrants could be appropriated by the firm with market power when it established the price of market access. The "conventional economic learning" as promulgated by the Chicago School said that since the profit-maximizing objective could always be accomplished by establishing the appropriate price of the use of the bottleneck, the only objective of a vertical foreclosure must be increased efficiency.

Note already that there is a tension between the conclusions one would draw from the Coase theorem and the permissive model of single firm behavior. While the former would assign a central role to the nature and presence of transactions costs in deciding the appropriate allocation of property rights, the latter assigns no discernible role to transactions costs but nevertheless reaches a determinate result, contrary to the Coase theorem.

However, Chapter 3 has shown that the permissive model of vertical foreclosures invoked in the rail industry is crucially dependent on the assumption that transactions costs are de minimis. If one is indifferent to the consequences for income distribution and willing to assume perfect information and no transactions cost to negotiations, any arbitrary market structure (even natural monopoly) can be shown to result in an efficient outcome in a narrow, short-term economic welfare sense. The welfare properties of the endowment of net income and its dynamic effects on concentration and competition, not short-run efficiency considerations, then paradoxically become the only consideration in the choice between alternatives. At a minimum, as Coase taught us, jurists and regulators need not worry about static efficiency considerations when they make judgments if transactions costs are zero.

The central role of transactions costs in the Coase theorem thus produces two possible real worlds, neither of which is likely to sit well with the Chicago School. If efficiency concerns are the principal rationale for judicial intervention into economic disputes, it must be because transactions costs are significant and a barrier to private negotiations to achieve the efficient results. If so, this can cut against the permissive approach to single firm behavior, which assumes that transactions costs may be safely ignored.

If de minimis transactions costs justify the permissive model, then the Coase theorem tells us that judges and regulators may safely ignore static efficiency concerns. While the Chicago School would hope that this would mean the repeal of laws justifying any regulatory intervention, this does not help those who must decide cases today. Indeed, the Coase theorem would stand the Chicago School story on its head. The Coase theorem tells judges to look only at considerations other than static efficiency in these circumstances, the exact opposite of the results hoped for by the proponents of the permissive model.

Things go even worse for the permissive model when it is realized that insignificant transactions costs may be inconsistent with the efficiency rationale for vertical foreclosures. Chapter 3 showed that the argument that the monopolist can always choose the profit maximizing price (and thus has no anticompetitive incentive to foreclose competition by unintegrated competitors) may conflict with the exclusive reliance on efficiency considerations to justify refusals to deal.

Of course, it may be argued that imperfect information and transactions costs block the exercise of the perfect price squeeze. If so, inefficient entrants may not be foreclosed via the pricing mechanism. But if true, this would undercut the conclusion that a monopoly profit was always available through the pricing mechanism and could not be enhanced via a foreclosure of competition.

Another tension is also driving these developments. While seeking to deny the existence of market imperfections that would justify various regulatory interventions into the market place, the permissive model cannot deny altogether the existence of market imperfections. The need to eliminate such imperfections could provide plausible explanations for behavior that would otherwise be labelled anticompetitive.

As noted in Chapter 2, the necessary fine tuning of assumed market imperfections can be very difficult. The market imperfections that are frequently cited as the source of efficiency gains are often the very same ones that permit anticompetitive vertical practices. The second leg of the paradox in these examples is that if the ability to achieve monopoly profits is satisfied via the pricing mechanism, as claimed, those prices will also foreclose inefficient market structures without the need for the vertical restriction (precisely because contestability will be degraded). In these applications, the theory of voluntary negotiations (which states that monopoly profits and static efficiency can always be achieved via bilateral negotiations over price) is simply inconsistent with the permissive theory of vertical foreclosures (which states that they can only be explained by efficiency motives).

Regulatory and judicial intervention into private economic matters ultimately depends on a clear understanding of the market imperfections that are present. Departures from perfect competition via the presence of transactions costs and sunk costs (departures from contestability) are likely to play a major role. Clarifying exactly what market imperfections are assumed to underlie the rationale for intervention must be the first step.

The assumption of hit-and-run entry has given an undeserved reputation of narrow applicability to the truly worthwhile contributions of contestability theory to multiproduct cost analysis and its determination of optimal industry structure. The undue emphasis on the assumption of contestability per se has obscured these valuable insights. Perhaps a moratorium on the use of both "contestability" and "ultra-free entry" (Shepherd 1984) to describe this larger body of work would be in order to encourage needed research to implement these useful costing concepts for the field of industry studies.

NOTE

1. Coase's (1960) original contribution was to note that the efficiency rationale for regulatory and legal intervention into disputes arises from the presence of transactions costs—the cost of negotiating and enforcing contracts that foreclose efficient contracts from solving these disputes. If the original rationale for regulatory intervention is no longer valid, the purpose of the thought experiment is to imagine the kinds of efficient contracts that would have been negotiated in the absence of regulatory intervention.

References

Aghion, Phillipe, and Patrick Bolton. 1987. "Contracts as a Barrier to Entry." *American Economic Review* 72, no. 3 (June): 388–401.

Alchian, Armen A., and William R. Allen. 1968. *University Economics*. Belmont, Calif.: Wadsworth Publishing Company.

Allen, W. Bruce. 1986. "Ramsey Pricing in the Transportation Industries." *International Journal of Transport Economics* 8, no. 3 (October): 293–330.

Anderson, David L., and William J. Rennicke. 1987. "The Contestable Market Defense: Measuring Competition in Freight Transportation." *Transportation Practitioners Journal* 54, no. 2 (Winter): 199–220.

Association of American Railroads (AAR). 1985. "Nation's Leading Economists Endorse Staggers." *Railway Age* (June): 32.

Bailey, Elizabeth E. 1981. "Contestability and the Design of Regulatory and Antitrust Policy." *American Economic Review* 71, no. 2 (May): 178–183.

Bailey, Elizabeth E., and William J. Baumol. 1984. "Deregulation and the Theory of Contestable Markets." *Yale Journal on Regulation* 1, no. 2: 111–137.

Bailey Elizabeth E., and Ann F. Friedlaender. 1982. "Market Structure and Multiproduct Industries." *Journal of Economic Literature* 20, no. 3 (September): 1024–1048.

Bailey, Elizabeth E., and John C. Panzar. 1981. "The Contestability of Airline Markets during the Transition to Deregulation." *Law and Contemporary Problems* 44, no. 1: 125–145.

Bailey, Elizabeth E., David R. Graham, and Daniel P. Kaplan. 1985. *Deregulating the Airlines*. Cambridge, Mass.: MIT Press.

Baumol, William J. 1977. "On the Proper Cost Tests for Natural Monopoly in a Multiproduct Industry." *American Economic Review* 67, no. 5 (December): 809–822.

———. 1979. "Minimum and Maximum Pricing Principles for Residual Regulation." *Eastern Economic Journal* 5, no. 1–2 (January): 235–248.

———. 1982. "Contestable Markets: An Uprising in the Theory of Industry Structure." *American Economic Review* 72, no. 1 (March): 1–15.

———. 1983a. Verified Statement in Finance Docket No. 30,300, *CSX Corporation—Control—American Commercial Lines, Inc.*, before the Interstate Commerce Commission, dated 4 November.

———. 1983b. "Some Subtle Pricing Issues in Railroad Regulation." *International Journal of Transport Economics* 10, no. 1–2 (April/August): 341–355.

———. 1983c. "The Apollo Reservation System and the Public Interest." *Comments of United Air Lines, Inc.*, Docket No. 41686, before the CAB, dated 17 November.

———. 1984a. "Some Subtle Pricing Issues in Railroad Regulation: Reply." *International Journal of Transport Economics* 11, no. 2–3 (August-December): 217–218.

———. 1984b. Verified Statement in Finance Docket No. 30,400, *Santa Fe Southern Pacific Corporation—Control—Southern Pacific Transportation Company: Merger—the Atchison, Topeka and Santa Fe Railway Company and Southern Pacific Transportation Company* (March) and Transcript pp. 10,083, 10,084, 10,091, and 10,198.

———. 1985a. Verified Statement in Finance Docket No. 30,400, *Santa Fe Southern Pacific Corporation—Control—Southern Pacific Transportation Company: Merger—the Atchison, Topeka and Santa Fe Railway Company and Southern Pacific Transportation Company*, dated 10 July.

———. 1985b. Verified Statement in Finance Docket No. 30,400, *Santa Fe Southern Pacific Corporation—Control—Southern Pacific Transportation Company: Merger—the Atchison, Topeka and Santa Fe Railway Company and Southern Pacific Transportation Company*, dated 21 February.

———. 1986a. Verified Statement in Docket No. 30,900, *Joint Application of CSX Corporation and Sea-Land Corporation under 49 U.S.C. 11321,* before the ICC, dated 14 July.

———. 1986b. "Williamson's *The Economic Institutions of Capitalism.*" *Rand Journal of Economics* 17, no. 2 (Summer): 279–286.

Baumol, William J., and David F. Bradford. 1970. "Optimal Departures from Marginal Cost Pricing." *American Economic Review* 60, no.3 (June): 265–283.

Baumol, William J., and Robert D. Willig. 1981. "Fixed Costs, Sunk Costs, Entry Barriers, and Sustainability of Monopoly." *Quarterly Journal of Economics* 96 (August): 405–431.

———. 1982. Verified Statement before the Interstate Commerce Commission, *Ex Parte* no. 347 (Sub-No. 1), *Coal Rate Guidelines—Nationwide*, 13 April.

———. 1983a. Verified Statement before the Interstate Commerce Commission, *Ex Parte* no. 347 (Sub-No. 1), *Coal Rate Guidelines: Nationwide*, 28 July.

———. 1983b. "Pricing Issues in the Deregulation of Railroad Rates." In *Economic Analysis of Regulated Markets*, ed. Jorg Finsinger. New York: St. Martin's Press.

———. 1985a. Verified Statement before the ICC, *Ex Parte* no. 456, *The Staggers Rail Act of 1980—Conference of Interested Parties*, 16 January.

———. 1985b. Verified Statement before the ICC, *Ex Parte* no. 445 (Sub-No. 1), *Intramodal Rail Competition*, 31 May.

———. 1985c. Reply Verified Statement before the ICC, *Ex Parte* no. 445 (Sub-No. 1), *Intramodal Rail Competition*, 8 July.

———. 1986a. "Contestability: Developments Since the Book." *Oxford Economic Papers* 38: 9–36.

———. 1986b. Testimony before the Railroad Accounting Principles Board, U.S. General Accounting Office, 18–19 June, Tr. 206–7.

Baumol, William J., Elizabeth E. Bailey, and Robert D. Willig. 1977. "Weak Invisible Hand Theorems on the Sustainability of Multiproduct Natural Monopoly." *American Economic Review* 67, no. 3 (June): 350–365.

Baumol, William J., John C. Panzar, and Robert D. Willig. 1982. *Contestable Markets and the Theory of Industry Structure*. New York: Harcourt Brace Jovanovich, Inc.

———. 1983. "Contestable Markets: An Uprising in the Theory of Industry Structure: Reply." *American Economic Review* 73, no. 3 (June): 491–496.

———. 1986. "On the Theory of Perfectly Contestable Markets." In *New Developments in the Analysis of Market Structure*, ed. Joseph E. Stiglitz and G. Frank Mathewson. Cambridge, Mass.: MIT Press.

Beilock, Richard. 1985. "Is Regulation Necessary for Value-of-Service Pricing?" *Rand Journal of Economics* 16, no. 1 (March): 93–102.

Bierce, Ambrose. 1958. *The Devil's Dictionary*. New York: Dover Publications.

Blair, Roger D., and David L. Kaserman. 1983. *Law and Economics of Vertical Integration and Control*. New York: Academic Press.

Boger, Daniel C. 1985. "Measuring Private and Social Cost in Inland Waterway Freight Transportation." In *Research in Transportation Economics* 2, ed. Theodore E. Keeler. Greenwich, Conn.: JAI Press.

Bonbright, James C. 1961. *Principles of Public Utility Rates*. New York: Columbia University Press.

Borenstein, Severin. 1985. "Price Discrimination in Free-Entry Markets." *Rand Journal of Economics* 16: 380–397.

Bork, Robert H. 1969. "Vertical Integration and Competitive Processes." In *Public Policy Toward Mergers*, ed. J. Fred Weston and Sam Peltzman. Pacific Palisades, Calif.: Goodyear Publishing Co.

———. 1978. *The Antitrust Paradox: A Policy at War with Itself*. New York: Basic Books.

Braeutigam, Ronald R. 1979. "Optimal Pricing with Intermodal Competition." *American Economic Review* 69, no. 1 (March): 38–49.

———. 1984. "Socially Optimal Pricing with Rivalry and Economies of Scale." *Rand Journal of Economics* 15, no. 1 (Spring): 127–134.

———. 1985. "Efficient Pricing with Rivalry between a Railroad and a Pipeline." In *Analytical Studies in Transport Economics*, ed. Andrew F. Daughety. Cambridge, England: Cambridge University Press.

Brand, Wallace E., and Daniel A. Leckie. 1984. "Wheeling Coal: An Antitrust Alternative to ICC Ratemaking." *Public Utilities Fortnightly* (30 August): 23–31.

Brock, William A. 1983. "Contestable Markets and the Theory of Industry Structure: A Review Article." *Journal of Political Economy* 91 (December): 1055–1066.

Cairns, Robert D., and Dhanayshar Mahabir. 1988. "Contestability: A Revisionist View." *Economica* 55, no. 218 (May): 269–276.

Call, Gregory D., and Theodore E. Keeler. 1985. "Airline Deregulation, Fares and Market Behavior: Some Empirical Analysis." In *Analytical Studies in Transport Economics*, ed. Andrew F. Daughety. Cambridge, England: Cambridge University Press.

Caves, Douglas W., Laurits R. Christensen, and Michael W. Tretheway. 1984. "Economies of Density Versus Economies of Scale: Why Trunk and Local Service Airline Costs Differ." *Rand Journal of Economics* 15 (Winter): 471–489.

Chamberlain, Edward H. 1933. *The Theory of Monopolistic Competition*. Cambridge: Harvard University Press.

Coase, R. H. 1960. "The Problem of Social Cost." *Journal of Law and Economics* 3 (October): 1–44.

Collins, William C. 1985. "Competitive Access Under Staggers." *Transportation Practitioners Journal* 52, no. 4 (Summer): 468–477.

Cook, James. 1987. "Open Access." *Forbes* (21 September): 48.

CSX Corporation. 1986. *Joint Application*, under 49 U.S.C. 11321, Docket No. 30,900 before the ICC, 14 July.

Cunningham, Paul A. 1986. As quoted in *Traffic World* (10 March): 15.

Damus, Sylvester. 1984. "Ramsey Pricing by U.S. Railroads: Can It Exist?" *Journal of Transport Economics and Policy* 18, no. 1 (January): 51–62.

Dasgupta, P., and J. E. Stiglitz. 1988. "Potential Competitors, Actual Competition and Economic Welfare." *European Economic Review* 32: 569–577.

Dewey, Donald. 1958. "Imperfect Competition No Bar to Efficient Production." *Journal of Political Economy* 66 (February): 24–33.

———. 1974. "The New Learning: One Man's View." In *Industrial Concentration: The New Learning*, ed. Harvey J. Goldschmid, H. Michael Mann, and J. Fred Weston. Boston, Mass.: Little, Brown and Company.

Dixit, Avinash, 1982. "Recent Developments in Oligopoly Theory." *American Economic Review* 72, no. 2 (May): 12–17.

Ekelund, Robert B., Jr., and Joe R. Hulett. 1973. "Joint Supply, the Taussig-Pigou Controversy and the Competitive Provision of Public Goods." *Journal of Law and Economics* 16: 369–387.

Faulhaber, Gerald R. 1975. "Cross Subsidization: Pricing in Public Enterprises." *American Economic Review* 65, no. 5 (December): 966–977.

Faulhaber, Gerald R., and William J. Baumol. 1988. "Economists as Innovators: Practical Products of Theoretical Research." *Journal of Economic Literature* 26, no. 2 (June): 577–600.

Fisher, Franklin M. 1979. "Diagnosing Monopoly." *Quarterly Review of Economics and Business* (Summer): 13.

Fitzroy, Felix R., and Dennis C. Mueller. 1984. "Cooperation and Conflict in Contractual Organizations." *Quarterly Review of Business and Economics* 24, no. 4 (Winter): 24–49.

Five Railroads, Comments of, before the Interstate Commerce Commission. 1983. *Ex Parte* no. 347 (Sub-No. 1), *Coal Rate Guidelines—Nationwide*, 28 July.

Frank, Robert H. 1983. "When Are Price Differentials Discriminatory?" *Journal of Policy Management and Analysis* (Winter): 238–255.

Friedlaender, Ann F., and Richard H. Spady. 1981. *Freight Transport Regulation*. Cambridge, Mass.: MIT Press.

Goldberg, Victor P. 1976. "Regulation and Administered Contracts." *Bell Journal of Economics* 7, no. 2 (Autumn): 426–448.

Graham, D. R., D. P. Kaplan, and D. S. Sibley. 1983. "Efficiency and Competition in the Airline Industry." *Bell Journal of Economics* 14 (March): 118–138.

Grimm, Curtis M. 1984a. *Preserving and Promoting Rail Competition*. Washington, D.C.: National Industrial Transportation League.

———. 1984b. "Promoting Competition in the Railroad Industry: A Public Policy Analysis." *Transportation Research Forum, Proceedings—Twenty-Fifth Annual Meeting*, 222–227.

Grimm, Curtis M., and Robert G. Harris. 1983. "Vertical Foreclosure in the Rail Freight Industry: Economic Analysis and Policy Prescriptions." *ICC Practitioners Journal* 50 (July–August): 508–531.

Huneke, William F., L. Lee Lane, and Thomas McNamara. 1985. "Greater Efficiency or Predation: The CSX-ACBL Merger." *Transportation Research Record 1038: Freight Papers—1985*. Washington, D.C.: Transportation Research Board.

Interstate Commerce Commission. 1983. *Ex Parte* no. 347 (Sub-No. 1), *Coal Rate Guidelines—Nationwide*, Decision dated 8 February.

Kahn, Alfred E. 1970. *The Economics of Regulation*, vol. 1. New York: John Wiley and Sons, Inc.

Kaplow, Louis. 1985. "Extension of Monopoly Power through Leverage." *Columbia Law Review* 85, no. 3 (April): 515–556.

Kaserman, David L. 1978. "Theories of Vertical Integration: Implications for Antitrust Policy." *Antitrust Bulletin* 23, no. 1: 483–510.

Keeler, Theodore E. 1983. *Railroads, Freight, and Public Policy*. Washington, D.C.: Brookings Institution.

Klein, Benjamin, Robert G. Crawford, and Armen A. Alchian. 1978. "Vertical Integration, Appropriate Rents, and the Competitive Contracting Process." *Journal of Law and Economics* 21, no. 2 (October): 297–326.

Krattenmaker, Thomas G., and Steven C. Salop. 1986. "Anticompetitive Exclusion: Raising Rivals Costs to Achieve Power over Price." *Yale Law Journal* 96, no. 2 (December): 209–293.

Landes, William M., and Richard A. Posner. 1981. "Market Power in Antitrust Cases." *Harvard Law Review* 94, no. 5 (March): 937–996.

Leibenstein, Harvey. 1966. "Allocative Efficiency versus *x*-efficiency." *American Economic Review* 56 (June): 392–415.

Lerner, Abba P. 1943. "The Concept of Monopoly and the Measurement of Monopoly Power." *Review of Economic Studies* (June): 157–175.

Levin, Richard C. 1981a. "Railroad Regulation, Deregulation, and Workable Competition." *American Economic Review* 72, no. 2 (May): 394–398.

———. 1981b. "Railroad Rates, Profitability, and Welfare under Deregulation." *Bell Journal of Economics* 12, no. 1 (Spring): 1–26.

Levine, Michael E. 1987. "Airline Competition in Deregulated Markets: Theory, Firm Strategy, and Public Policy." *Yale Journal on Regulation* 4, no. 2: 393–494.

Locklin, D. Phillip. 1933. "The Literature on Railway Rate Theory." *Quarterly Journal of Economics* 47 (February): 167–230.

Marshall, Charles N., and Cheryl A. Cook. 1986. "Issues of Cost Recovery in the Debate over Competitive Access." *Transportation Law Journal* 15, no. 1: 9–31.

Mas-Colell, Andrew. 1982. "Noncooperative Approaches to the Theory of Perfect Competition: Presentation." In *Noncooperative Approaches to the Theory of Perfect Competition*, ed. Andrew Mas-Colell. New York: Academic Press.

McFarland, Henry. 1987. "The Economics of Vertical Restraints and Relationships between Connecting Railroads." *Logistics and Transportation Review* 23, no. 2 (June): 207–222.

Meyer, John R., and William B. Tye. 1985. "The Regulatory Transition." *American Economic Review* 75, no. 2 (May): 46–51.

———. 1988. "Toward Achieving Workable Competition in Industries Undergoing a Transition to Deregulation." *Yale Journal on Regulation* 5, no. 2 (Summer): 273–297.

Morrison, Steven A., and Clifford Winston. 1986. *The Economic Effects of Airline Deregulation*. Washington, D.C.: Brookings Institution.

———. 1987. "Empirical Implications and Tests of the Contestability Hypothesis." *Journal of Law and Economics* 30 (April): 53–66.

National Association of Attorneys General. 1985. *Vertical Restraints Guidelines* (4 December), as reported in Bureau of National Affairs, *Antitrust and Trade Regulation Report* 49: 996–1010.

Ordover, Januz A., and Robert D. Willig. 1983. "The 1982 Department of Justice Merger Guidelines: An Economic Assessment." *California Law Review* 71 (March): 571.

Ordover, J. A., A. O. Sykes, and R. D. Willig. 1985. "Nonprice Anticompetitive Behavior by Dominant Firms toward Producers of Complementary Products." In *Antitrust and Regulation*, ed. Franklin M. Fisher. Cambridge, Mass.: MIT Press.

Panzar, John C. and Robert D. Willig. 1977a. "Free Entry and Sustainability of Natural Monopoly." *Bell Journal of Economics* 8, no. 1 (Spring): 1–22.

———. 1977b. "Economies of Scale in Multi-Output Production." *Quarterly Journal of Economics* 91, no. 3 (August): 481–493.

———. 1981. "Economies of Scope." *American Economic Review* 71, no. 2 (May): 268–272.

Perry, Motty. 1984. "Sustainable Positive Profit Multiple-Price Strategies in Contestable Markets." *Journal of Economic Theory* 32: 246–265.

Phillips, Almarin. 1975. "Schwinn Rules and the 'New Economics' of Vertical Market Relations." *Antitrust Law Journal* 44: 573.

———. 1980. "Ramsey Pricing and Sustainability with Interdependent Demands." In *Regulated Industries and Public Enterprise*, ed. Bridget M. Mitchell and Paul R. Kleindorfer. Lexington, Mass.: D. C. Heath and Company.

Posner, Richard A. 1969. "Natural Monopoly and its Regulation." *Stanford Law Review* (February): 548–643.

———. 1978–1979. "The Chicago School of Antitrust Analysis." *University of Pennsylvania Law Review* 127: 925–948.

Quirmbach, Herman C. 1982. "Vertical Integration, Contestable Markets, and the Misfortunes of the Misshaped U." Unpublished paper, Rand Corporation, P–6782, June.

Rey, Patrick, and Jean Tirole. 1986. "The Logic of Vertical Constraints," *American Economic Review* 76, no. 5 (December): 921–939.

Salinger, Michael A. 1988. "Vertical Mergers and Market Foreclosure." *Quarterly Journal of Economics* 103, no. 2 (May): 345–356.

Samuelson, Paul A. 1947. *Foundations of Economic Analysis*. Cambridge, Mass.: Harvard University Press.

Scherer, R. M. 1980. *Industrial Market Structure and Economic Performance*. Chicago: Rand-McNally.

Schmalensee, Richard. 1979. "On the Use of Economic Models in Antitrust: The ReaLemon Case." *University of Pennsylvania Law Review*, 1005, 1011.

———. 1982. "Another Look at Market Power." *Harvard Law Review* 95 (May): 1789–1816.

Schwartz, Marius. 1986. "The Nature and Scope of Contestability Theory." *Oxford Economic Papers* 38 (November suppl.): 37–57.

Schwartz, Marius, and Robert J. Reynolds. 1983. "Contestable Markets: An Uprising in the Theory of Industry Structure: Comment." *American Economic Review* 73, no. 3 (June): 488–490.

Shepherd, William G. 1984. " 'Contestability' v. Competition." *American Economic Review* 74, no. 4 (September): 572–587.

———. 1986. "Illogic and Unreality: The Odd Case of Ultra-Free Entry and Inert Markets." In *Antitrust and Regulation*, ed. Ronald E. Grieson. Lexington, Mass.: Lexington Books.

———. 1988. "Competition, Contestability, and Transport Mergers." *International Journal of Transport Economics* 15, no. 2 (June): 113–128.

Sherman, Roger and Anthony George. 1979. "Second Best Pricing for the U.S. Postal Service." *Southern Economic Journal* 45 (January): 685–695.

Simon, Herbert A. 1978. "Rationality as Process and as Product of Thought." *American Economic Review* 68, no. 2 (May): 1–16.

Spence, Michael. 1983. "Contestable Markets and the Theory of Industry Structure: A Review Article." *Journal of Economic Literature* 21, no. 3 (September): 981–990.

Spencer, Barbara J., and James A. Brander. 1983. "Second Best Pricing of Publicly Produced Inputs: The Case of Downstream Imperfect Competition." *Journal of Public Economics* (February): 113–119.

Spengler, Joseph. 1950. "Vertical Integration and Antitrust Policy." *Journal of Political Economy* 58 (July/August): 347–354.

Stiglitz, Joseph E. 1981. "Potential Competition May Reduce Welfare." *American Economic Review* 71, no. 2 (May): 184–189.

———. 1987. "Technological Change, Sunk Costs, and Competition." *Brookings Papers on Economic Activity*, vol. 3. Washington, D.C.: Brookings Institution, 883–937.

Troy, Daniel E. 1983. "Unclogging the Bottleneck: A New Essential Facility Doctrine." *Columbia Law Review* 83, no. 2 (March): 441–487.

Tye, William B. 1983. "Balancing the Ratemaking Goals of the Staggers Rail Act." *Transportation Journal* 22, no. 4 (Summer): 17–26.

———. 1984a. "Revenue/Variable Cost Ratios and Market Dominance Proceedings." *Transportation Journal* 24, no. 2 (Winter): 15–30.

———. 1984b. "The Role of Revenue/Variable Cost Ratios: Determinations of Rail Rate Reasonableness." *Proceedings: Transportation Research Forum* 25, no. 1: 214–221.

———. 1984c. "Some Subtle Pricing Issues in Railroad Rate Regulation: Comment," and "Rejoinder." *International Journal of Transport Economics* 11, no. 2–3 (August-December): 207–216, 219–220.

———. 1984d. "On the Effectiveness of Product and Geographic Competition in Determining Market Dominance." *Transportation Journal* 24, no. 1 (Fall): 5–19.

———. 1984e. "Financing the Stand-Alone Railroad." *Logistics and Transportation Review* 19, no. 4: 291–308.

———. 1985a. "The Applicability of the Theory of Contestable Markets to Rail/Water Carrier Mergers." *Transportation and Logistics Review* 21, no. 1 (March): 57–76.

———. 1985b. "Problems of Applying Stand-Alone Costs as an Indicator of Market Dominance and Rate Reasonableness." *International Journal of Transport Economics* 12, no. 1 (February): 7–30.

———. 1986a. "Stand-Alone Costs as an Indicator of Market Dominance and Rate Reasonableness." *International Journal of Economics* 13, no. 1 (February): 21–40.

———. 1986b. "Preserving Post-Merger Rail Competition via the Parity Principle." *Transportation Journal* 26, no. 2 (Winter): 39–54.

———. 1986c. "Post-Merger Denials of Competitive Access and Trackage Rights in the Rail Industry." *Transportation Practitioners Journal* 53, no. 4 (Summer): 413–427.

———. 1986d. "Rate Base and Rate of Return Methodologies for Determining Reasonable Rates for Captive Rail Traffic." *Transportation Research* 20A, no. 1 (January): 1–14.

———. 1987a. "The Contestable Market Defense in Freight Antitrust Cases." *Transportation Practitioners Journal* 54, no. 2 (Winter): 177–198.

———. 1987b. "Pricing Rail Competitive Access in the Transition to Deregulation with the Revenue/Variable Cost Test." *Antitrust Bulletin* 32, no. 1 (Spring): 101–135.

———. 1987c. "The Voluntary Negotiations Approach to Rail Competitive Access in the Transition to Deregulation." *Antitrust Bulletin* 32, no. 2 (Summer): 415–450.

———. 1987d. "Competitive Access: A Comparative Industry Approach to the Essential Facility Doctrine." *Energy Law Journal* 8, no. 2: 337–379.

———. 1987e. "The Contestable Market Defense in Freight Antitrust Cases." *Transportation Practitioners Journal* 54, no. 2 (Winter): 177–198.

———. 1988. "Pricing Trackage Rights to Achieve Post-Merger Rail Competition." *Logistics and Transportation Review* 24, no. 4 (December): 318–348.

———. 1989. "Incentive Compatibility of the Revenue/Variable Cost Test for Rail Competitive Access." *Antitrust Bulletin* 34, no. 1 (Spring): 153–184.

Tye, William B., and Herman Leonard. 1983. "On the Problems of Applying Ramsey Pricing to the Railroad Industry with Uncertain Demand Elasticities." *Transportation Research* 17A, no. 6 (November): 439–450.

U.S. Court of Appeals for the District of Columbia. 1984. *Coal Exporters Association of the United States et al.* v. *Interstate Commerce Commission* 745 F.2d 76 (D.C. Circuit).

U.S. Department of Justice. 1985. *Vertical Restraints Guidelines*, 23 January, as cited in Bureau of National Affairs, *Antitrust and Trade Regulation—Report* 48, no. 1199: 3–12.

U.S. Department of Transportation. 1985. Comments before the Interstate Commerce Commission, in *Ex Parte* no. 445 (Sub-No. 1) (31 May): 19.

U.S. General Accounting Office. 1987. "Railroad Regulation: Competitive Access and Its Effects on Selected Railroads and Shippers." Washington, D.C., June, GAO/RCED–98–109.

Warren-Boulton, Frederick. 1978. *Vertical Control of Markets*. Cambridge, Mass.: Ballinger Publishing Company.

Waterson, Michael. 1982. "Vertical Integration, Variable Proportions, and Monopoly." *Economic Journal* 92 (March): 129–144.

Weiss, Nitzan, and Phil Lee. 1986. "Sustainability of the Multiproduct Monopoly and Ramsey Optimal Pricing." *Journal of Institutional and Theoretical Economics* 142: 473–492.

Weitzman, Martin L. 1983. "Contestable Markets: An Uprising in the Theory of Industry Structure: Comment." *American Economic Review* 73, no. 3 (June): 486–487.

Westfield, Fred M. 1981. "Vertical Integration: Does Product Price Rise or Fall?" *American Economic Review* 71, no. 3 (June): 334–346.

Wheeler, Porter K., and Ronald L. Friedland. 1986. "Joint Rate Cancellations Since the Staggers Rail Act of 1980." *Proceedings—Transportation Research Forum*, 122–130.

Williamson, Oliver E. 1974. "The Economics of Antitrust: Transaction Cost Considerations." *University of Pennsylvania Law Review* 122: 1439.

———. 1975. *Markets and Hierarchies: Analysis and Antitrust Implications*. New York: Free Press.

———. 1979. "Assessing Vertical Market Restrictions: Antitrust Ramifications of the Transaction Cost Approach." *University of Pennsylvania Law Review* 127, no. 4 (April): 953–993.

———. 1985. *The Economic Institutions of Capitalism*. New York: Free Press.

Willig, Robert D. 1979a. "The Theory of Network Access Pricing." In *Issues in Public Utility Regulation*, ed. Harry M. Trebing. East Lansing, Mich.: Michigan State University, Graduate School of Business Administration.

———. 1979b. "Multiproduct Technology and Market Structure." *American Economic Review* 69, no. 2 (May): 346–351.

———. 1980. "What Can Markets Control?" In *Perspectives on Postal Service Issues*, ed. Roger Sherman. Washington, D.C.: American Enterprise Institute.

———. 1981. "Economies of Scope." *American Economic Review* 71, no. 2 (May): 268–272.

———. 1983. Verified Statement in Docket No. 37850S. *Mobil Chemical Company* v. *Seaboard System Railroad, Inc.* 3 June.

———. 1984a. Verified Statement in Docket No. 38279S et al. *Detroit Edison* v. *Consolidated Rail Corporation et al.* 13 February.

———. 1984b. Verified Statement in Docket 39176 (Sub-No. 1). *Pittsburgh and Lake Erie Railroad* v. *Conrail*. 5 March.

Willig, Robert D., and William J. Baumol. 1987. "Using Competition as a Guide." *Regulation*, no. 1: 28–35.

Wilson, Wes W., Frank Dooley, Gene C. Griffin, and Ken Casavant. 1986. "The Applicability of the Theory of Contestable Markets to Railroad Competition." *Proceedings—Twenty-Seventh Annual Meeting, Transportation Research Forum* 27, no. 1: 131–136.

Index

About the Author

WILLIAM B. TYE is an expert in industrial economics and the author of *Encouraging Cooperation among Competitors: The Case of Motor Carrier Deregulation and Collective Ratemaking*.